James Balog

Copyright © 1988 Collins Publishers, Inc., New York

First published 1988

All rights reserved. No part of this publication may be repro-
duced, stored in a retrieval system, or transmitted in any form
or by any means, electronic, mechanical, photocopying, recor-
ing or otherwise, without prior written permission of the
publisher.

ISBN 0-00-217967-9

Library of Congress Cataloging-in-Publication Data
Main entry under title: A Day in the Life of Spain

1. Spain—Description and travel—1981—Views
2. Spain—Social life and customs—Pictorial works
I. Smolan, Rick
II. Cohen, David, 1955-
III. Title

DP43.2.D513 1988 946.083′022′2 87-21836

British Library Cataloging-in-Publication Data
Main entry under title: A Day in the Life of Spain

1. Spain—Social life and customs—1951—Pictorial works

946.083′022′2 DP48

Project Directors: Rick Smolan and David Cohen

Art Director: Thomas K. Walker

Designer: Jim Stockton

Printed in Spain by Cayfosa, Santa Perpétua
de Mogoda, Barcelona

Separations by Arnoldo Mondadori Editore,
Verona, Italy

First printing: February 1988

10 9 8 7 6 5 4 3 2 1

A Day in the Life of Spain

Photographed by 100 of the
world's leading photojournalists
on one day, May 7, 1987

Collins Publishers

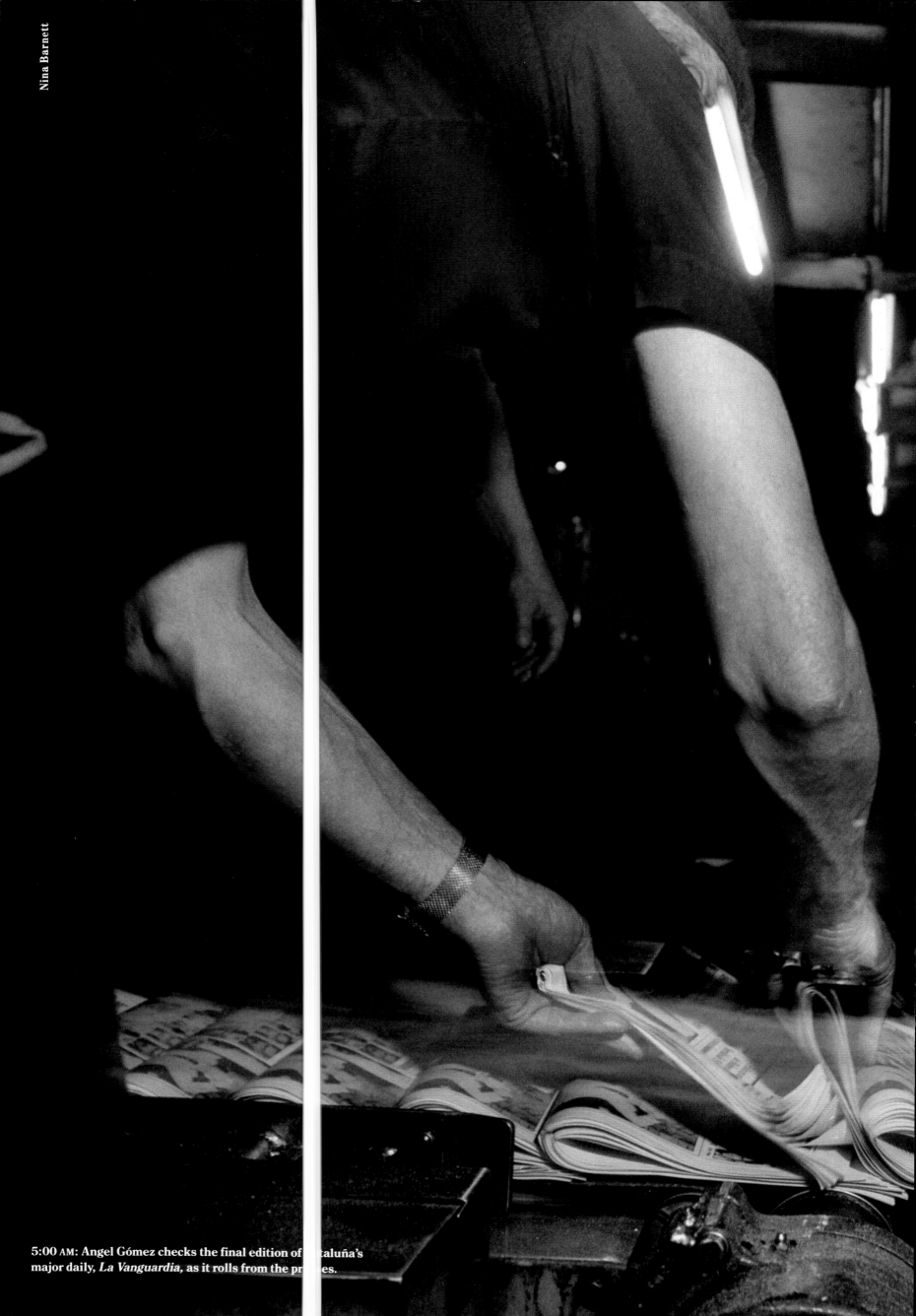

5:00 AM: Angel Gómez checks the final edition of Cataluña's major daily, *La Vanguardia,* as it rolls from the presses.

5:30 AM: A morning hose-down for one of the 53 trains that depart daily from Abando station in Bilbao

6:00 AM: A farmer walks through the dawn mist along the banks of the Ulla River in Galicia, a favorite spot for local

Spain. España. The name conjures up visions: hot, dusty plazas and statues of *conquistadores* under the siesta sun; La Mancha's white windmills—their vanes slowly spinning above the Castilian plain; flamenco dancers—backs arched, heels clicking a furious staccato; the swirl of a matador's cape and the blood of the bull as it drops to its knees.

Except that we are in the Spain of the 1980s—May 7, 1987, to be precise. And instead of deserted, sun-baked plazas, we find bustling boulevards crowded with fashionable shoppers and savvy businessmen. The windmills of La Mancha are here, but modern-day Quixotes are converting them into vacation homes. The young boy sleeping under a bullfight poster may someday don the matador's "suit of lights," but he may just as well end up a *punk* wearing a uniform of jeans, studded leather and live rodents. Flamenco is still alive and kicking, but stroll through a different door and you'll find hundreds of young people gyrating to the beat of "la Movida," an intoxicating mix of art, fashion and just plain exuberance that is turning Madrid into the *enfant terrible* of Europe.

This is Spain today, seen through the piercing eyes of 100 top photographers who freeze-framed the nation during a mad 24-hour exposure. *A Day in the Life of Spain* captures the country I knew while Madrid correspondent for *The New York Times*—the old and the new, side by side in metamorphic flux; a country fairly exploding out of four decades of isolation and dictatorship. For Spain—"that arid square, that fragment nipped off from hot Africa, soldered so crudely to inventive Europe," as W.H. Auden put it—is belatedly pulling itself out of the 19th century and rushing headlong into the 21st. The businessmen on the Barcelona-Madrid air shuttle, the woman public relations executive applying makeup on the fly as she rushes to work, the young couple kissing in the public square in Vitoria—all of these belong to the new, modern, liberal Spain.

Yet the old, traditional country lives close by the new. Look closely at the old men in berets sharing a thought, the widow dressed in lifelong black, the farmer and his hand-held Roman plow. This is ancient, imperial, proud Spain, with enough traces of grandeur to make a day's passing feel like a century's.

The world-weary photojournalists returned from the Spain shoot wide-eyed with delight at its bounties. Through their photographs it is easy to see why they so quickly became passionate about España and its people.

—John Darnton

Un día en la Vida de
ESPAÑA

March 1, 1987

Dear Photographer,

I'm an American freelance photographer, and for the past ten years I've been working on assignments around the world for magazines including *Newsweek, Time, Fortune, The* London *Sunday Times, Stern* and *National Geographic.* I'm writing to invite you to work on a project that David Cohen and I are organizing here in Madrid.

This is what we have in mind: We want to position 100 of the world's best photographers throughout Spain and give each photographer the same 24-hour period to capture a typical Spanish day on film. The results of this 24-hour shoot will be a hardcover book called, "A Day in the Life of Spain."

Spain has gone through an extraordinary transformation since Franco's death. Spain today is a country led by a generation of politicians in their thirties and forties, probably the youngest group of political leaders in Europe. In the past decade, this country has become one of Europe's most exciting cultural centers. It has also become the world's most popular tourist destination with more than 47 million visitors last year.

The goal of the "Day in the Life of Spain" project is to show the world how Spain has changed and to generate a great deal of national pride within Spain itself. We hope to accomplish this by asking people throughout Spain to join our 100 professional photographers by photographing their own family and friends during the course of the same day (May 7, 1987).

With his Majesty King Juan Carlos and Prime Minister Felipe Gonzalez have agreed to participate as photographers on the day. Their participation will help turn this project into an event that will touch the lives of millions of Spaniards. Of all the projects we have ever put together, "A Day in the Life of Spain" appears to have the greatest potential for turning a book project into a nationwide event.

The "Day in the Life of Spain" project has several purposes: First and foremost to create a superior photographic document that may answer a few questions about Spain and perhaps ask a few more; to involve the Spanish people in a nationwide celebration of photography; to allow you and the other photojournalists to share the camaraderie which has characterized previous "Day in the Life" projects; and finally, to provide a group of talented individuals with the opportunity to work together on a collaborative project.

On Saturday, May 2, 1987, you and other leading photojournalists from 20 countries will arrive in Madrid. On Thursday May 7, 1987, each of you will photograph a specific aspect of Spanish life. All over the country, 100 photographers will race against the clock to freeze Spain on film during the course of a single day.

We are not setting out to make the definitive statement about Spain nor to cover the entire country in a single day. That would be impossible. Nor will we concentrate on the rich, the famous or the powerful. Instead, we will ask you to apply your skills to one of the toughest jobs in photojournalism: to make extraordinary photographs of ordinary, everyday events.

la Joan Miro, Palacio de Congresos, Paseo de la Castellana 99, Madrid 28046.
Tel: 456 3111   Fax: 456 3801

We will give each of you a specific assignment, but you will also have the freedom to shoot whatever you discover by accident on the day -- the assignment is just a starting point. All we ask is that you make great pictures.

If all goes well, the project will produce a large format hardcover book, a one-hour television special, a calendar featuring the best photographs from the project and a traveling exhibit of photographic prints.

Although this project is made possible by Eastman Kodak, Iberia Airlines, Renfe, Telefonica, Campsa, McDonnell Douglas, Avis Rental Car, Apple Computer, the Palace Hotel, the Instituto Nacional de Promocion del Tourismo and a number of other corporations, it is not a public relations exercise or a tourist promotion. All of the supporters of the project understand that you are a journalist and that they will have no editorial control over what you shoot or what is selected for the book. We want "A Day in the Life of Spain" be an honest look at Spain in the 1980s, not just another book of pretty picture postcards.

By the same token, there is no guarantee that every photographer will get a picture in the book. That depends on whether or not you have a good day on May 7th.

At the moment, the 40 of us on staff are frantically putting the last pieces in place to make sure everything goes smoothly when you and the other photographers arrive. If working with us on this crazy idea appeals to you, here are a few things you will need to know and a few things we need from you very quickly:

1) **Biography:** Don't be modest. We need as much information as possible about your photography career -- awards, exhibits, books published, etc.

2) **Film:** Kodak will supply you with 50 rolls of film (Kodachrome 64 or 200 or T-MAX-400). It would help us to know your film requirements in advance.

3) **International Transportation:** You will be provided with a round-trip ticket from your home city to Madrid courtesy of Iberia Airlines. Iberia will also fly you from Madrid to your assignment location.

4) **Ground Transportation:** If your assignment requires it, you will be provided with a free rental car courtesy of Avis Rental Car.

5) **Roommates:** If you take advantage of the hotel rooms provided to you courtesy of The Palace Hotel, you will share a twin room with a famous photographer at absolutely no extra charge.

6) **Payment:** All expenses including air and ground travel will be covered by us. In return for the one day of shooting, you have the choice of receiving either a cash honorarium of $1,000 or an Apple Macintosh Plus computer system and Imagewriter 11 printer.

There is no question that this will be an extremely challenging project. Although we have done "Day in the Life" projects in Australia, Hawaii, Canada, Japan and America, this will be the first time that we have tried the concept in Europe and we are not sure the idea will translate. This is a risky project. We need people of your calibre and experience to ensure that this book will be as successful as our first five "Day in the Life" books.

We hope you will be able to lend your skills, and believe you will be as fascinated with Spain as we are.

Best regards,

Rick Smolan

Rick Smolan

● *Previous pages 14-15*

Early morning light streams through the Crystal Palace, the gem of Madrid's elegant Retiro Park. Built in 1887 to display exotic plants from the Philippines, a former Spanish colony, it is now used for art exhibitions.
Photographer:
Brennon Jones, USA

● *Previous pages 16-17*

Peace of the Rock: Angel Sánchez ends a night of shellfishing on the Bay of Algeciras as the sun catches Britain's Rock of Gibraltar. Spain has claimed the strategic enclave at the entrance to the Mediterranean ever since the British took possession in 1713. Generalissimo Francisco Franco sealed the frontier between the rock and the Spanish town of La Línea de la Concepción for more than a decade, but now hundreds of Spaniards work in Gibraltar.
Photographer:
Larry C. Price, USA

arely awake, Beatriz Moreno
e Silva, seven, waits for her
ounger sister, Catalina, to join
er for breakfast. The girls
nd their parents live in a 15th-
entury manor house on a
,500-acre *cortijo*, or ranch, near
e village of Palma del Río, the
irthplace of the great matador
l Cordobés.
Photographer:
odi Cobb, USA

● *Left*

Briton Geoffrey Dobson wel-
comes the Mediterranean sun-
rise with a cup of tea at his
beach-front apartment in El
Perelló, just south of Valencia.
Dobson left England 12 years
ago, joining some 80,000 other
Britons who have migrated
permanently to the warm Spanish *costas*.
Photographer:
Eric Lars Bakke, USA

● *Above*

Smiles greet Mercedes López
as she treats the family to breakfast in bed in their El Ferrol,
Galicia, home. López says that
her husband, Ricardo, a worker
at the local Bazán shipyards,
sometimes does the honors.
Photographer:
**José María Alguersuari,
Spain**

● *Left*

Windmills guard the castle of Consuegra, 70 miles south of Madrid in the heart of Don Quixote's La Mancha. In a modern tilt, some affluent men of La Mancha are now turning the windmills into weekend homes.
Photographer:
Georg Gerster, Switzerland

● *Above*

Saddle-up: At Zaragoza Military Academy, Spain's officer training school, cadets face morning inspection. Among the academy's alumni are King Juan Carlos and Crown Prince Felipe. New York photographer Misha Erwitt reported that life for the 600 cadets was more relaxed than it is at West Point: "They have wine at lunch and hang around their own bar in the evening. In the United States, you really catch it if you drink anywhere near the military academy."
Photographer:
Misha Erwitt, USA

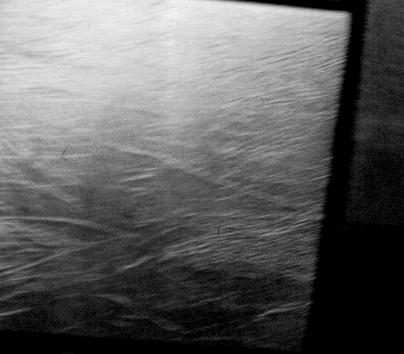

● *Left*

The briefcase brigade sets off on the 8:30 AM *puente aéreo,* the Iberia Airlines shuttle that flies between Madrid and Barcelona, Spain's commercial capitals. Nearly 3,000 businessmen a day hop the shuttle, and most agree that the 12-year-old service has done more to link the tradition-ally competitive cities than any other government initiative.
Photographer:
Bernardo Pérez, Spain

● *Above*

Thirty-four-year-old Amelia Noriega, head of public relations for ENASA, a major Spanish truck manufacturer, prepares for another day as one of Spain's top women executives. "There aren't many women at my job level in Spain," she says. (Only 21 of ENASA's 760 supervisors are female.) "But there are more every day."
Photographer:
Angel Ruiz de Azúa, Spain

● *Previous pages 24-25*

On Iberia's Barcelona-Madrid
shuttle: One million passengers
a year make this 45-minute
flight, the most profitable do-
mestic route for Spain's national
carrier.
Photographer:
Bernardo Pérez, Spain

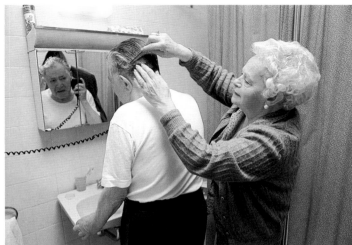

● *Left*

Public relations executive
Amelia Noriega applies a
last-minute touchup while com-
muting to her executive suite
at ENASA.
Photographer:
Angel Ruiz de Azúa, Spain

● *Above*

Retired hairdresser Elena Las-
peñas, 76, lends a professional
hand to her husband, Victorino,
at the Casa de Misericordia, a
home for senior citizens in
Pamplona.
Photographer:
Stephanie Maze, USA

● *Previous pages 28-29*

Bus stop: Children of Itero de la Vega, in Castilla-León, run for the school bus that takes them to classes in nearby Astudillo.
Photographer:
Pedro Coll, Spain

● *Left*

Jesús Suárez, 73, displays fruit and vegetables at the shop he and his wife, Pepita Ricote, 75, run on Madrid's Barquillo Street. Business was better when Pepita's father opened the store 80 years ago. The more affluent customers have moved to the suburbs, and the couple now caters mostly to senior citizens.
Photographer:
Angel Ruiz de Azúa, Spain

● *Above*

In Melilla, a Spanish toehold on Morocco's North African coast, Moslem women shop for produce imported daily from mainland Spain. A Spanish possession for nearly 500 years, Melilla is an ethnically mixed community of 60,000 with an estimated 27,000 Moslems.
Photographer:
Jean-Pierre Laffont, France

● *Left*

Slice of life: Eighty-year-old Josefa Albiol dresses a 345-pound tuna in the Boquería, Barcelona's central market. By closing time, she had sold the entire fish. A fishmonger since she was eight, Josefa shares the family stall with her son, Jaime, and his wife, María Luisa, who rise at 3:00 every morning to purchase their stock at the Mercabarna wholesale fish market. Jaime is teaching his 17-year-old daughter the trade, just as he was taught by his mother. Since Spaniards eat an average of 84 pounds of fish each year, the Albiol family has a fine future in fish-selling.
Photographer:
Paul Chesley, USA

● *Above*

Home on the range: These old Spanish Air Force transports have been put out to pasture.
Photographer:
Ethan Hoffman, USA

● *Previous pages 34-35*

San Francisco photographer George Steinmetz arrived at his assignment in Barcelona, Spain's second-largest city, expecting "fishing boats, cows in the pastures and old ladies." Instead, he was struck by how modern, industrialized and sophisticated the Catalán capital is. Perhaps as a metaphor, Steinmetz decided to photograph Barcelona's most recognizable landmark, the spires of Antonio Gaudí's Sagrada Familia cathedral, framed by TV antennas, laundry and a construction crane.

Photographer:
George Steinmetz, USA

● *Left*

Though she's shown hanging sheets out to dry, Mercedes, 31, spends much of her time running the bar she owns in downtown Sevilla. Drying laundry is rarely a problem in this city, where midsummer temperatures often exceed 100 degrees.
Photographer:
Peter Turnley, USA

● *Above*

Young Francisco Martínez feeds the doves in Valencia's Plaza de la Virgen.
Photographer:
Víctor Steinberg, Spain

● *Above*

Satala Sou peers from his hide-out, an abandoned garage near the port of Las Palmas in the Canary Islands. Sou, one of hundreds of Africans who stow away to the Canaries each year, arrived two months ago from Nigeria aboard a Korean fishing vessel and sneaked ashore at night. While looking for a ship that will take him to a northern European port, he earns money scrubbing the decks of freight-ers that put into Spain's busiest international port.

Spanish photographer Juantxu Rodríguez says, "Sou's most treasured possession is a snap-shot of his wife and two children. He said he didn't mind having his picture taken because he expected to be far away by the time *A Day in the Life of Spain* is published."
Photographer:
Juantxu Rodríguez, Spain

● *Right*

When the sun shines in Asturias, northwest Spain, housewives rush to hang out the morning wash. In one of the country's wettest regions, a fine day can-not be wasted.
Photographer:
José María Alguersuari, Spain

● *Above*

Stockbrokers jostle for position during frenzied midmorning buying and selling on the floor of *la Bolsa,* Madrid's stock exchange.
Photographer:
Rich Clarkson, USA

● *Right*

Brokers at Madrid's *la Bolsa* take a break between 15-minute trading sessions. Unlike most international exchanges, *la Bolsa* permits only one block of stock to be traded at a time. Founded in 1831, it is the largest of Spain's four stock exchanges and accounts for 82 percent of the nation's trading.
Photographer:
Rich Clarkson, USA

● *Left*

A riverboat ferries a shift of steelworkers across Bilbao's Nervión River to the Altos Hornos de Vizcaya steel mill. The plant now operates at half capacity, a victim of declining demand.
Photographer:
Diego Goldberg, Argentina

● *Above*

Migrant worker María Díaz greets *Day in the Life* photographer Gary Chapman with a box of strawberries she picked at the Santa María de la Rábida cooperative farm in Palos de la Frontera. Spain's "strawberry revolution" was sparked by the introduction of scientifically improved strains during the 1980s. These dramatically changed the economy of this village and others in the southwestern part of the country.

Before the strawberry boom, "all Palos produced was hunger, and people had to emigrate to find jobs," says the cooperative's director, José Luis Gutiérrez. "Now we have to import workers." The cooperative expects to gross $32 million this year.
Photographer:
Gary S. Chapman, USA

Georg Gerster

O ver La Mancha, where Don Quixote dreamed his impossible dream, Swiss aerial photographer Georg Gerster discovered unimaginable scenes. "The landscape overwhelms," he says. "I knew it would be good, but I didn't know it would be this good."

La Mancha, a vast plateau that unfolds south of Madrid, has a magic all its own. It forms the southern part of the *meseta,* a 2,000-foot-high tableland that is the heart of the Iberian peninsula. Horizons are limitless, population is sparse and rainfall is scarce.

Says Gerster, "I used to think that Spain was, for my way of seeing the world, the most beautiful country in Europe. And now I know it."

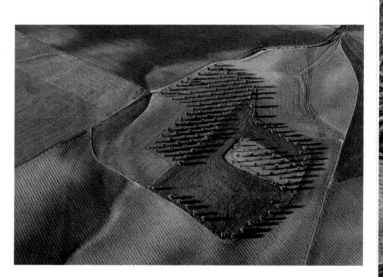

● *Above*

Near Ciudad Real: An island of wheat and olives is surrounded by a sea of newly planted grapevines. Half of Spain's wine flows from the La Mancha region.
Photographer:
Georg Gerster, Switzerland

● *Right*

Near Toledo: These terraced hills were once cultivated by the Romans.
Photographer:
Georg Gerster, Switzerland

● *Previous pages 44-45*

Over Toledo province: Olive
trees cast shadows on wheat
fields and vineyards.
Photographer:
Georg Gerster, Switzerland

● *Right*

Above the province of Ciudad
Real: A field is ready for
planting.
Photographer:
Georg Gerster, Switzerland

101234
56789

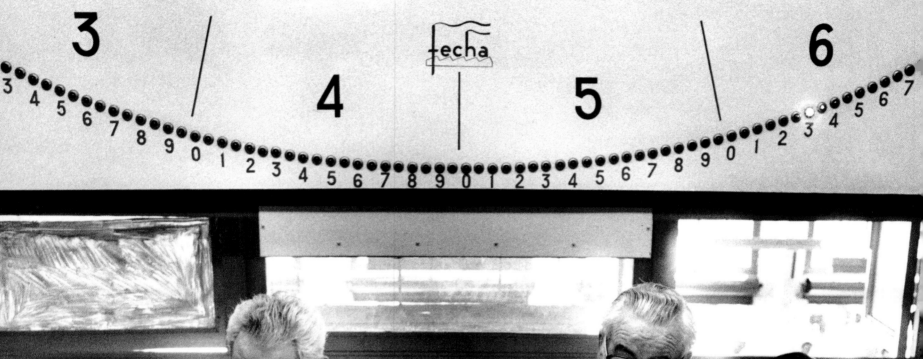

3 / 4 fecha 5 / 6

3456789012345678901234567890123456789012345 67

● *Left*

Fresh sardines are auctioned at the dockside headquarters of the Fishermen's Association in Bermeo, the Basque region's largest fishing port. The giant wheel behind the auctioneers indicates the fluctuating prices for the day's catch.
Photographer:
Andy Levin, USA

● *Above*

Isabel Pérez, 56, and Encarna Franco, 49, harvest potatoes on a *huerta,* or small farm, in Murcia, one of Spain's most fertile regions. During the spring potato harvest, the women earn around $18 per day. The rest of the year, they pick cotton, beans, artichokes and a variety of citrus fruits.
Photographer:
Arnaud de Wildenberg, France

● *Following pages 50-51*

Carmen Sotelo, a laundress at the Massó fish cannery in Cangas, Galicia, hangs towels to dry in the early morning. The fish-canning business in this northwest region of Spain is more than a century old.
Photographer:
Sarah Leen, USA

● *Above*

Members of the Ertzaintza, the Basque regional police force, practice a riot-control exercise at their training academy near Vitoria, the seat of the Basque autonomous government. After the death of Generalissimo Franco in 1975, the Basque country, Cataluña and certain other Spanish regions won more administrative authority from the central government, including expanded law-enforcement powers.
Photographer:
Robin Moyer, USA

● *Right*

Banking high over the plain of Aragón, a Spanish Air Force F-18 heads for home at Zaragoza Air Base. *Washington Post* photographer Frank Johnston mounted a camera inside the cockpit of the McDonnell Douglas fighter and asked the copilot to push the shutter release.

Johnston reported a near disaster while placing the camera: "They told me not to touch anything with a yellow and black stripe in the cockpit because it would trigger the ejection seat. And what do I do? I carefully step on the pilot's seat and my elbow hits a yellow-and-black-striped lever. The fellow in the back seat starts yelling, 'My God, watch out! You're going to eject me!'" Fortunately the pilot stayed put, and Johnston got his shot.
Photographer:
Frank Johnston, USA

● *Following pages 56-57*

A courtyard in the maximum-security prison at Herrera de la Mancha, south of Madrid. Some 220 convicted terrorists from the Basque separatist organization ETA (an acronym for Euskadi ta Azkatasuna, or Basque Homeland and Liberty) are serving sentences here of between 10 and 30 years.

When *Day in the Life* photographer Ethan Hoffman came to take pictures on May 7th, each cell block voted on whether it would cooperate. Three out of four refused. Still, Hoffman, who has photographed several US prisons, was impressed: "These are not your typical prisoners. They are disciplined, and the level of violence is low. Conditions are better than those in any prison I saw in the States."
Photographer:
Ethan Hoffman, USA

Ethan Hoffman

● *Below*

Clutching their guide rope, kindergarten children are led to the playground through a maze of narrow streets in the medieval town of Vich, in Cataluña.
Photographer:
Carlos de Andrés, Spain

● *Above*

Outside Moncloa Palace, camera-shy María gets a hug from her father, 45-year-old Spanish Prime Minister Felipe González.
Photographer:
Lynn Goldsmith, USA

● *Right*

Seventh-grader Alvaro González writes a passage from *Don Quixote* on a blackboard in the Madrid suburb of Entrevías. Alvaro, an aspiring matador, is as passionate as Don Quixote himself when it comes to bull-fighting. "I want to be a bull-fighter more than anything else in the world," says the youth, who spends four hours each afternoon studying at Madrid's bullfighting school in hopes of becoming a millionaire matador. Alvaro could be fighting professionally by the time he is 17. Says photographer Mark Wexler, "He's a wonderful boy who's trying to make it big in bullfighting to get his family out of a poor economic situation."
Photographer:
Mark S. Wexler, USA

The face behind the mask: Daniel, nine, offers a shoulder to his cousin Teresa, 11. Nicknamed "El Gallo" or "Rooster," Daniel is a family breadwinner. Each day at dawn, the youngster leaves Ripollet gypsy encampment for Barcelona to beg and wash the windshields of stopped cars. Like most kids in the gypsy community, neither Daniel nor Teresa attends school.
Photographer:
Mary Ellen Mark, USA

S pain's 500,000 *gitanos,* or gypsies, don't drive brightly colored horse-drawn caravans down bucolic country lanes. They live in decrepit high-rise apartments or squalid shantytowns. They are Spain's pariahs—outcasts from one of Europe's fastest-growing economies. "We live in the Third World," says Manuel Martín, leader of a *gitano* rights group.

Nonetheless, New York photographer Mary Ellen Mark found an upbeat mood at a gypsy encampment outside the town of Ripollet, near Barcelona. The camp consists of rusting trailers and makeshift sheds next to a river that floods in winter. Mark says, however, that the site "didn't feel like a refugee camp. It was orderly and clean inside the caravans. There was lots of laughter."

Few among the 1,000-strong community hold regular jobs, and most are illiterate. Like *gitanos* throughout the country, they scrounge a living collecting refuse, washing car windows, selling lottery tickets and trading in open-air markets. Most gypsy families have four or five children (double the national average), and the street-smart kids, who rarely attend school, soon become valuable breadwinners. Government efforts to provide decent housing and education for gypsies have proved controversial since any attempt to incorporate *gitanos* into Spanish society usually meets a wall of racial prejudice.

● *Left*

A team of art restorers touches up panels at Las Huelgas monastery in Burgos. Founded 800 years ago, the monastery is undergoing rehabilitation, including restoration of its paintings, icons and carvings.
Photographer:
Neal Ulevich, USA

● *Above*

Francisco de Goya's "La Maja Desnuda" ("The Maja Undressed") is scrutinized by an art lover at Madrid's Prado museum. Legend has it that the painting is of the Duchess of Alba, reputedly Goya's lover, but that the artist painted the face of her maid to spare the duchess embarrassment. Housing one of the richest art collections in the world, the Prado opened to the public in 1819 and is now visited by four million people a year.
Photographer:
John Loengard, USA

● *Above*

Lucio Maire clings to the scaffolding high inside the chapel of the monastery of Las Huelgas in Burgos. Maire and 29 others have spent four years restoring the monastery, which was built by Alfonso VIII in 1187. Maire's mask and special clothing protect him from noxious chemicals used in the restoration process.
Photographer:
Neal Ulevich, USA

● *Right*

Rafael Mazarrasa, 39, civil governor of the province of Cuenca, a mountainous terrain east of Madrid. "Cuenca is typical of the Castilian region," says Mazarrasa. "It's arid but has surprisingly fertile zones and beautiful, rich areas of woodland." Mazarrasa, a onetime radical student leader at Madrid University, has worked to promote the arts in his sparsely populated province.
Photographer:
Raphaël Gaillarde, France

● *Following pages 72-73*

The Barcelona stock exchange is Spain's second largest, after Madrid's, and traces its history to 1401, when merchants first swapped royal bonds. May 7th proved to be a bad day at the Barcelona market. Concern over the debt burdens of Spanish utilities caused a major drop in stock values.
Photographer:
Paul Chesley, USA

Paul Chesley

● *Above*

Welders at the state-owned Astano shipyard near El Ferrol in northwest Spain: Astano has dropped 4,000 of its 6,200 workers since 1971 and is shifting its business to the production of oil-drilling platforms.
Photographer:
Xurxo Lobato, Spain

● *Right*

The biggest moneymaker in this Toledo stationery shop isn't pens and pencils but church-blessed statues of the infant Jesus that Julián Torres (left) and Remedios Fernández sell for as much as $36. They are a must for relatives of children celebrating their first communion.
Photographer:
Dilip Mehta, Canada

● *Below*

Two nuns enjoy a stroll along one
of Toledo's more fashionable
streets.
Photographer:
Dilip Mehta, Canada

● *Above*

End of the line: Mexican photographer Graciela Iturbide came across this trio while strolling through Santiago de Compostela, in Galicia.
Photographer:
Graciela Iturbide, Mexico

● *Right*

Taking the bull by the horns: Joaquín Moreno de Silva, 35, gets by with a little help from his friend. The son of Alonso Moreno de la Coba, one of Spain's top breeders, he is inspecting a wound inflicted on a young cow's back by a picador during a *tienta*, or testing. If the animal responds to the testing with bravado, she will be kept for breeding purposes. Otherwise, it's off to the butcher. As *National Geographic* photographer Jodi Cobb put it, "It's either motherhood or hamburger."
Photographer:
Jodi Cobb, USA

Don't be sheepish: Antonio
Moles, a farmer in the Pyrenees
village of Campo, is determined
to drag this ewe to the shearer.
Photographer:
Jay Dickman, USA

King Juan Carlos and Queen Sofía leave Zarzuela Palace in their bulletproof Mercedes. The king is touching up a speech he will deliver at the Royal Academy, the distinguished council on the Spanish language.

After more than 30 years of authoritarian rule, Spanish dictator Francisco Franco handpicked the exiled young prince as his successor in 1969. Juan Carlos was left with the task of reuniting a badly fragmented nation and guiding it to democracy. Surprisingly, and against all odds, he has largely succeeded. Photographer and *Day in the Life* co-director Rick Smolan says, "I've photographed many heads of state but few like this. His foremost concern was to put me at ease."

Photographer:
Rick Smolan, USA

Miners descend into the heart of an Asturias coal mine in Sama de Langreo. At one point, photographer Sam Garcia put aside his cameras: "I actually worked the coal face with a pneumatic drill. I figured it wasn't fair to be there and not know what it was like to do the work."

Photographer:
Sam Garcia, USA

● *Left*

A sickle and a scythe: These farm laborers are on one of the many large, privately owned farms near Marinaleda, in southern Andalucía. The sickle may be as symbolic as practical for farmers in Marinaleda. Most of the town's landless agricultural workers are particularly radical and organized along Communist lines in a bid to change land ownership in the region.
Photographer:
Koldo Chamorro, Spain

● *Above*

Workmen spray a final coat of varnish on a coffin at their plant in Mora de Ebro, Cataluña. The coffin factory produces one line that sells for under $100. The luxury model, priced at $800, is called the "Kennedy."

Photographer Eduardo Martínez was one of the winners of the *Day in the Life of Spain* photo contest, held for the Spanish public on May 7th.
Photography contest winner:
Eduardo Martínez, Spain

● *Above*

On the Canary Island of Lan-
zarote, which has more than 300
inactive volcanoes and only eight
hours of rain per year, farmers
like Miguel Rosa have devised a
unique form of agriculture. They
grow crops in deep craters that
protect them from the wind and
enable their roots to reach below
the volcanic crust in search of
water. The volcanic ash also acts
like a sponge, collecting precious
night moisture to sustain plants
during the sun-baked day.
Photographer:
Carlos Navajas, Spain

● *Right*

Small boats in the inner harbor
of San Sebastián on the Bay of
Biscay in northern Spain.
Photographer:
Dan Dry, USA

● *Above*

May 7th was a somber day on several political fronts: In the Cantabrian town of Reinosa, sullen crowds attend the funeral of laminator Gonzalo Ruiz, who died three weeks after being injured in a clash with police at a local steel plant. Ruiz, 32, was hit by a rubber bullet and tear-gassed when police broke up a protest against planned job cuts.
Photographer:
Dominique Mollard, France

● *Right*

In the Basque country, Félix Peña, a victim of the region's polarized politics, is carried through the streets of Portugalete by fellow members of the Socialist party. Peña, 55, was killed in a firebomb attack on the party's local headquarters. The attack was blamed on Basque extremists, who advocate greater self-rule and independence from the Socialist government in Madrid.
Photographer:
Diego Goldberg, Argentina

● *Left*

Dressed in traditional black, an old woman tends to the niche of a loved one in the Cangas cemetery in Galicia. In many rural areas of Spain, widows don black as a sign of mourning and continue to wear it, almost as a uniform, for the rest of their lives.

Photographer:
Sarah Leen, USA

● *Above*

José Gordillo, flanked by his wife, his son and a friend, places a casket containing the bones of his brother into a small repository at Sevilla's San Fernando cemetery. Limited burial space and, until recently, a Catholic church ban on cremations led to this Spanish burial practice. Bodies are first placed in a normal, full-length coffin. Once the corpse has decomposed, the family opens the coffin and transfers the remaining bones to a smaller box, which is then placed in a sepulchre. Wealthy families avoid the process by buying a plot of land and building a mausoleum.

Photographer:
Peter Turnley, USA

● *Above*

In El Cerro de Andévalo, Apolonia Serrano, 21, brightens up the feast of Saint Benedict, a week-long religious festival that dates back to the 16th century. More than just a fiesta-stopper, Serrano's hat contains a saintly relic.

Photographer:
Cristina García Rodero, Spain

● *Right*

In the bag: Pabi Astondoa trains for an upcoming sack-lifting contest. Sack-lifting has recently joined scything and wood-chopping as a competitive sport in the Basque region. A week after this picture was taken, the first sack-lifting competition was held in Astondoa's village of Ceánuri. He won handily, lifting a 220-pound sack 44 times in three minutes.

Photographer:
Galen Rowell, USA

● *Above*

Travel agent and amateur photographer José Román Guilartte happened upon this contest-winning shot in Granada's Albaicín quarter. "We're progressing," says Guilartte about the sign on the shoe repair door. "It says 'Back in 10 minutes.' In the past it would have said 'Back mañana.'"

Photography contest winner:
José Román Guilartte, Spain

● *Right*

Barber Matias Sánchez gives a haircut to 12-year-old Alvaro González (last seen on pages 60-61). Alvaro, a promising student at Madrid's school for matadors, hopes someday to earn the $30,000 per fight that the best bullfighters make. And he knows what he would do with such wealth: "I'd make sure my mother doesn't have to clean other people's homes." Unlike Alvaro, 19th-century bullfighters wore a long pigtail that was cut only when they retired.

Photographer:
Mark S. Wexler, USA

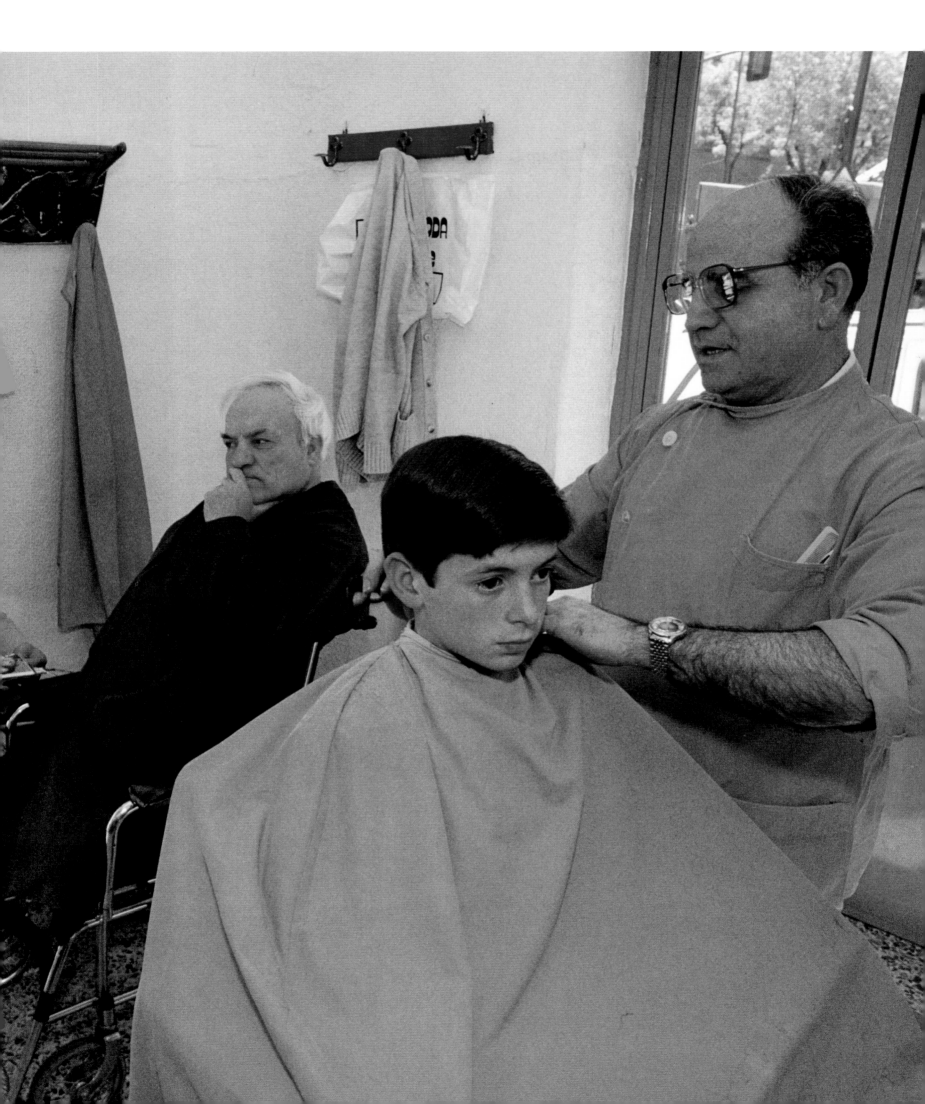

● *Above*

Nine-year-old Jesús Alberto García will wear this new sailor suit at his first communion, a ritual celebrated by almost every Spanish child. (Girls wear more formal attire, usually a miniature bridal gown.) The Garcías will pay about $100 for this outfit at Murcia's largest department store, part of the El Corte Inglés chain. The store says it sells some 2,000 first communion outfits yearly.

Photographer:
Miguel González, Spain

● *Right*

A Spanish punk, or *punky* as they are known locally, draws stares on a Bilbao sidewalk. Punks are a common urban phenomenon throughout Spain, but in Bilbao and other Basque cities they are more politicized, often supporting the extremist separatist movement.

Photographer:
Robb Kendrick, USA

Left

Left

May 7th was fiesta day in El Cerro de Andévalo. Excitement mounted as the *mayordomos,* or town stewards, walked through the village handing out cakes and candy to the crowd.
Photographer:
Cristina García Rodero, Spain

• *Left*

Young British arrival: Four-year-old Katie Coles peers out the front door of her new home in the village of Teguise, in the Canary Islands. Katie, who recently moved with her family from England, is one of many Britons who have established residence in Spain.
Photographer:
Carlos Navajas, Spain

Basilio Perona Cortés, Age 13   S. Adrián Besós, Cataluña

Irantzu Chinchetru, Age 9   Vitoria, Basque country

Bernardo M. Ramos González, Age 9   Gomera, Canary Islands

Miriam Bellido Mora, Age 12   Madrid

Mónica de Miguel Vázquez, Age 11   Madrid

Nicolás Pascual Equisvany, Age 8   Barcelona, Cataluña

Daniel López Azaña, Age 8   Móstoles, Madrid

Ana María Arias Rodríguez, Age 8   Madrid

María López Pedreján, Age 10   Itero de la Vega, Castilla-León

Pedro P. Porto Taboada, Age 12   La Estrada, Galicia

María López Pedreján, Age 10   Itero de la Vega, Castilla-León

Agustín Montes García, Age 8   Madrid

● *Left*

It's known as a *tertulia* and it's a Spanish tradition. Close friends meet regularly to chat at a café or bar. These gents sit at the same table every evening at Nuevo Casino, a private Pamplona club founded in 1868. Their conversations must be interesting, since the group includes a landowner, a cattle dealer, a government official, a tax inspector and a professor of Greek.

Photographer:
Stephanie Maze, USA

● *Above*

Calculated to please: Mathematics professor Francisco Soto, 64, checks his paella, a traditional Valencian dish of rice, shellfish, meat, vegetables and saffron. Soto's culinary masterpiece won rave reviews from his family and *Day in the Life* photographer Patrick Tehan.

Photographer:
Patrick Tehan, USA

● *Above*

Javier de Juan, a 29-year-old painter and illustrator, is preparing a major one-man show for the fall. De Juan typifies "la Movida," Madrid's hip cultural movement of the 1980s, which translates roughly as "the Happening." Gallery owner Isabel Garrigues, one of de Juan's patrons, says, "I don't know if 'la Movida' will stay with us, but what we have at the moment is the youthful spirit of Spain saying something valuable, saying it well and saying it now."

Photographer:
Nicole Bengiveno, USA

● *Right*

Antonio López, 51, at work in his Madrid studio, is one of Spain's most famous contemporary painters. López has established his reputation with one-man shows in New York, London, Paris and other art capitals.

Photographer:
Miguel Bergasa, Spain

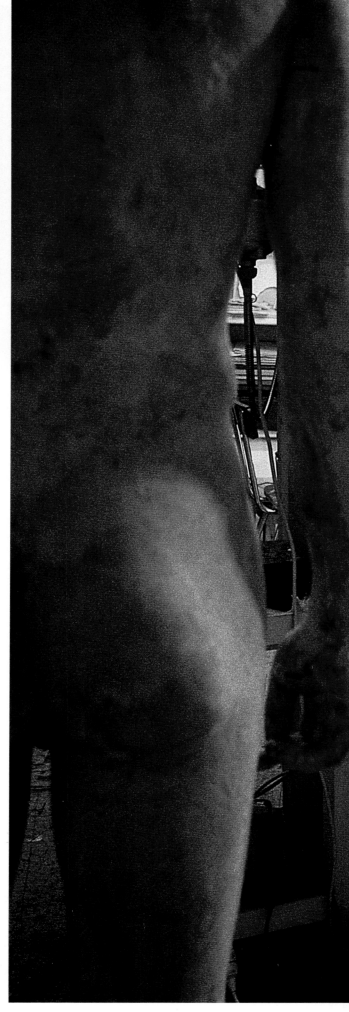

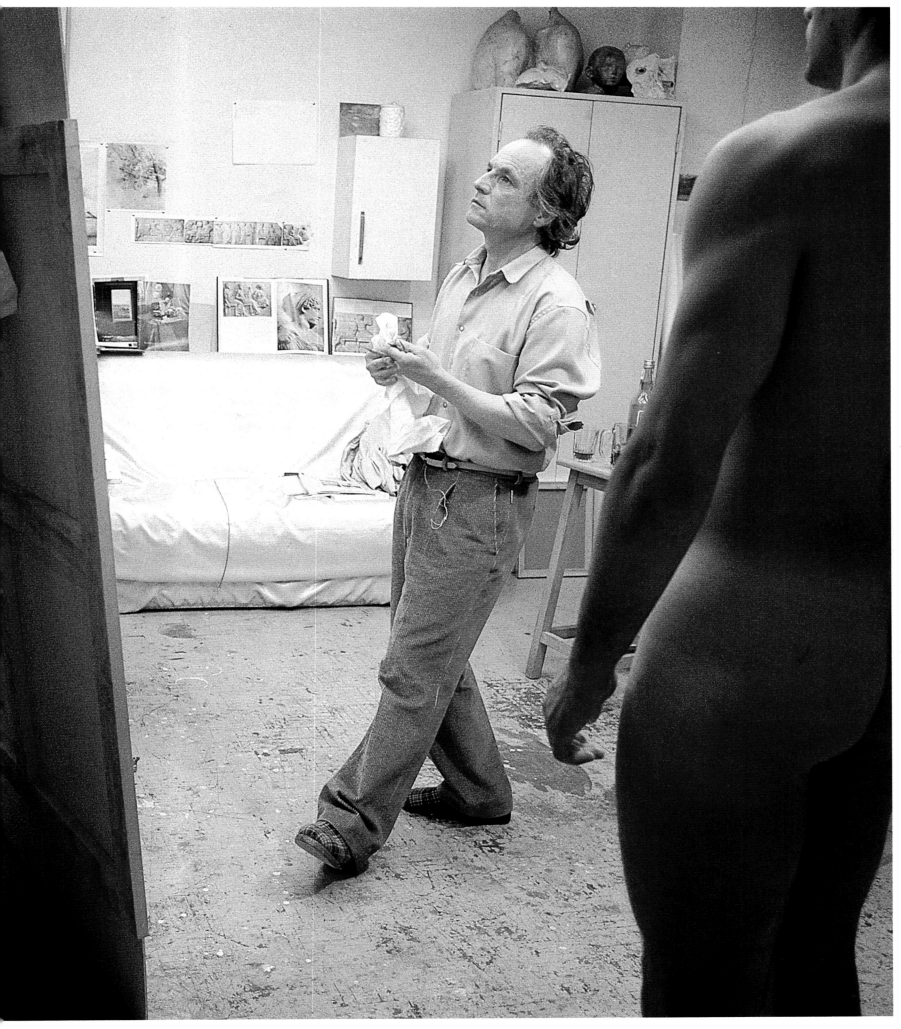

Guardia Civil patrol, in tradi-
onal tricornered hats, guards
s barracks above the town of
llafranca de Ordizia. A para-
ilitary force of 60,000 men, the
uardia Civil has been battling
dical Basque separatists since
e mid-1960s. Only 10 months
rior to May 7th, these barracks
ffered a grenade attack.

Aside from its peacekeeping
nctions, the Guardia Civil
olices transport routes, custom

houses and penitentiaries. Created in 1844 to combat rural
banditry in southern Spain, it
suppressed pockets of resistance
after the Falangist victory in the
Spanish Civil War and maintained
national discipline during the
Franco years.
Photographer:
Jerry Gay, USA

In a mock exercise at their Gua-
dalajara training camp, members
of Spain's elite antiterrorist unit
prepare to blast their way into a
building containing hostages.
The GEO, or Special Operations
Group, is similar to British and
American quick-response anti-
terrorist groups.
Photographer:
**Manuel Hernández de León,
Spain**

● *Previous pages 108-109*

Workers at the ENASA truck factory in Madrid's eastern industrial belt take a break from the assembly line for a bite and a quick squirt or two.
Photographer:
Angel Ruiz de Azúa, Spain

● *Left*

A barrel of Rioja is rolled to the decanting area at the Muga winery in Rioja province. Rioja is stored in giant wooden vats for a year, and egg whites are added to remove sediment. It is then transferred to barrels and aged for an additional two to four years before being bottled. The winery likes to use American oak for its barrels and vats because of the distinctive flavor it imparts.

Photographer:
Andrew Stawicki, Canada

● *Above*

Ventura Muñoz swigs water from a *botijo,* a traditional earthenware jug. Muñoz and his team are adjusting the angle of the 2,000 panels in a 230-foot-wide NASA tracking dish. One of only three such stations in the world, the Robledo de Chavela facility, near Madrid, was receiving images from the US Voyager mission headed toward Neptune on May 7th.

Photographer:
Adam Lubroth, USA

● *Previous pages 114-115*

El Toboso, the home of Dulcinea, Don Quixote's lady love: In the 16th century, it boasted a population of 20,000. Today El Toboso is a quietly prosperous agricultural village of just over 2,000.
Photographer:
Georg Gerster, Switzerland

● *Left*

A boy runs through the Moslem neighborhood of Hidum in the city of Melilla on Morocco's Mediterranean coast. Melilla has been a Spanish enclave for nearly 500 years.
Photographer:
Jean-Pierre Laffont, France

● *Above*

Retired farmworkers Justo Senosiaín, 80, and Fernando Egea, 78, chat at the bar of the Casa de Misericordia, a Pamplona home for senior citizens.
Photographer:
Stephanie Maze, USA

● *Below*

Andalusian horses race for the pasture. A forerunner of the Texas ranch horse, the *caballo andaluz* was imported to the Americas by the *conquistadores* and played a key role in the Spanish colonization of the New World. These thoroughbreds are part of a herd of 200 and sell for up to $160,000 apiece.
Photographer:
Jodi Cobb, USA

● *Left*

Holiday sunsoakers head home from Puerto Rico beach on Gran Canaria, off the northwest coast of Africa. When Europeans go on vacation, they tend to go to Spain. More than 3.5 million tourists (mostly English, French, German and Scandinavian) visit the Canaries each year, and more than 40 million unwind throughout Spain, making it the world's top tourist destination. In 1986, tourism earned the country $12 billion, 9 percent of its gross national product.

Photographer:
Arthur Grace, USA

● *Above*

Downside up: *Day in the Life of Spain* contest winner Joaquim Cabezas i Rectoret recorded his wife, María, 52, suntanning on the roof of their Tarragona apartment house.

Photography contest winner:
Joaquim Cabezas i Rectoret, Spain

Out-of-work Marinaleda farm laborer Antonio Conejo and his family eat a lunch of *cocido*, a

ern region of Andalucía. Conejo, like most laborers in the area, can count on only two solid

3:15 PM

● *Above*

King of Spain Juan Carlos trains his lens on the royal family. The popular monarch is an avid photographer and owns more than a dozen cameras.
Photographer:
Fernando Sacristán, Spain

● *Right*

King Juan Carlos, an experienced pilot, positions his craft close to a Spanish Air Force Chinook helicopter in the skies over Toledo province. The military transport was carrying a six-ton abstract sculpture from artist Eduardo Chillida's studio near Madrid to a spot overlooking the ancient city of Toledo.
Photographer:
Rick Smolan, USA

● *Right*

Royal snap: Queen Sofía is flanked by Princess Cristina, 22, who is studying political science at Madrid University, and Princess Elena, 23, who teaches at a primary school. On May 7th, Prince Felipe, the 19-year-old heir to the throne, was aboard a Spanish Navy clipper ship in the Caribbean.
Photographer:
H.M. Juan Carlos, King of Spain

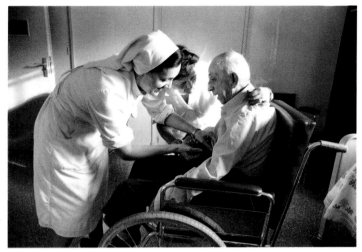

Everyone knows about the running of the bulls in Pamplona, but few people know that the bulls are running for a good cause. Pamplona's senior citizens can retire comfortably at Casa de Misericordia (House of Charity) because the old-age home owns the town's famous bullring and receives more than $1 million each year from bullfight tickets. The 584 residents are cared for by 163 staff members, and photographer Stephanie Maze was impressed by their dedication. "It seemed like an extended family," she says. "I hope I'm that well taken care of when I'm their age."

At left, retired farmworker Román Espinosa, 82, is attended by social worker Felisa Iriarte (center) and nurse Teresa Martínez.
Photographer:
Stephanie Maze, USA

● *Left*

Iriarte joins a conversation between the Casa's oldest residents, Prudencia Peiró, 105, and Rosa Pajares, 108 (center). "Rosa was very soft-spoken and gentle," Maze recalls, "and Prudencia was feisty. You could see she was a fighter when she was younger."
Photographer:
Stephanie Maze, USA

● *Above*

Reflective moment: Former shopkeeper Isabel Alfonso, 87, sits in the dining hall.
Photographer:
Stephanie Maze, USA

● *Left*

The spires of the Sagrada Familia, Antonio Gaudí's unfinished Barcelona cathedral, encircle José María Subirachs. Subirachs is the sixth sculptor-architect to tackle the herculean task started by Barcelona's renowned architect in 1882. Gaudí died in a streetcar accident in 1926, and since then construction on the Sagrada Familia has continued in fits and starts. Subirachs, 60, expects to spend 15 years sculpting the 100 or so 13-foot figures that will decorate the north face of the church. He calls the Sagrada Familia "the work of a lifetime" but doubts that he will see it finished.

Photographer:
Paul Chesley, USA

● *Above*

Holy accounting: Benedictine nuns in a convent near Madrid adjusted to a financial pinch by purchasing computers and processing the accounts of local companies. Recalls American photographer Anne Day, "When I first entered the convent—it was unbelievable—three rows of nuns were hard at work on their computers. Without stopping, they just looked up and, smiling, sang a Gregorian chant while they typed."

Photographer:
Anne Day, USA

● *Left*

José and Alfredo Cadenas search for one of their 12 dairy cows near their home in Piornedo, a remote section of Galicia. In winter, the hamlet is often snowed in and its 16 families must be supplied by helicopter. Belgian photographer John Vink found the Piornedans to be "secretive at first but very open-hearted once you get to know them."
Photographer:
John Vink, Belgium

● *Above*

María Escudero, Spain's "Miss Turismo 1987," is at an exhibit of traditional flamenco dresses in Córdoba.
Photographer:
Tomasz Tomaszewski, Poland

● *Previous pages 132-133*

Miguel Benito, a member of
Spain's Guardia Civil, walks his
nine-year-old son, David, home
from school. The Benito family
lives in a fortified barracks near
the Basque village of Villafranca
de Ordizia. Resentment against
the national Guardia Civil is
strong in the Basque region, so
Benito and his colleagues seldom
leave the barracks without their
weapons.
Photographer:
Jerry Gay, USA

● *Above*

A waiter rests his feet in one of
the more elegant bars of Cuenca.
Photographer:
Raphaël Gaillarde, France

● *Below*

A farmer rides his mule to work
in the fields below La Calahorra
castle in Guadix. Once the prin-
cipal draft animals and transport
for rural Spaniards, mules have
declined in population from over
a million in 1960 to only 130,000.
The 16th-century castle, near
Granada, is empty, but locals
hope it will soon be converted
into a tourist hotel.
Photographer:
**Claus C. Meyer,
West Germany**

● *Above*

A 70-foot fighting bull dominates
the highway near Córdoba. One
hundred twelve of the two-
dimensional beasts, trademarks
for Osborne wineries, are
placed strategically along major
Spanish roads.
Photographer:
Tomasz Tomaszewski, Poland

● *Right*

Spain's top breeder of fighting
bulls, Victorino Martín, takes a
siesta at a ranch hand's cottage.
Martín's 1,700-acre spread is in
the western region of Extrema-
dura. He started raising bulls
for the ring in 1968 and now
maintains a herd of 550. His
1,200-pound *toros* sell for about
$6,500 each and enter the ring
at between four and five years
of age.
Photographer:
Skeeter Hagler, USA

● *Left*

The game is called *brisca,* and the next round of drinks will be bought by the holder of the losing hand. A simplified form of canasta played with a Spanish deck of 40 cards, the game helps these senior citizens of Campo de Criptana pass the time. The retirees, all long-standing friends in this La Mancha city of 13,000, play in a social center built by the local savings bank.

Photographer:
James Balog, USA

● *Above*

Waiting for a five: A dominoes player guards his wager in a café in Itero de la Vega. Dominoes is a popular pastime, and many rural bars provide sets for their customers.

Photographer:
Pedro Coll, Spain

● *Below*

Father Pablo spoons incense into
a censer during early morning
mass at Santa María de Sobrado
monastery.
Photographer:
Benito Román, Spain

Since 1142, daily life at Santa María de Sobrado monastery has begun at 5:00 AM with 40 minutes of plainchant and ended at 10:00 PM with evening prayer. Twenty-five Cistercian monks—the oldest is 80, the youngest 25—live at the medieval abbey situated in a Galician valley 40 miles north of Santiago de Compostela. Spanish photographer Benito Román was warmly welcomed by the monks but nonetheless found it a bit of a shock to meet people who live a contemplative life in "such a solid, almost invulnerable place."

The monastery has, in fact, had mixed fortunes. Midway through the 19th century, during the Carlist civil wars, the monks were forced to flee the friary, and they didn't reclaim the cloister until the mid-1960s. Today the community includes a small dairy farm, a vegetable garden and a sausage and hamburger factory.

The monks also tried to run a drug rehabilitation center for local addicts but, according to Father Superior Salvador, "decided that good will was not enough." Now the brothers stick to farming and run a 30-room guest house, fully booked months in advance, for visitors on retreat.

● *Above*

He usually strums classical tunes, but today Father Luis works out some chords from a recent Dire Straits hit.
Photographer:
Benito Román, Spain

● *Right*

Father Antonio slices potatoes for dinner.
Photographer:
Benito Román, Spain

142

● *Right*

Artist-in-residence: Father
Jaime is the icon painter at Santa
María de Sobrado. He sells most
of his work to tourists but gives
some to his fellow monks.
Photographer:
Benito Román, Spain

On May 7th, Tour of Spain cyclists raced from El Ferrol to La Coruña, in the hilly, green countryside of Galicia, in northwest Spain. One of the toughest cycling events in the world (along with the Tour de France and the Giro d'Italia), the Vuelta Ciclista lasts 22 days and courses the length and breadth of the country. Cyclists peddle an average of 111 miles per day, and only half of the 200 or so who start will cross the finish line in Madrid.
Photographer:
José María Alguersuari, Spain

Antonio Valladeras, chief cook at Barcelona's Salmonete Restaurant, keeps a customer waiting while he watches, along with millions of other enthusiasts throughout Spain, a close moment in the Vuelta Ciclista as it winds through the Galician countryside.
Photographer:
Nina Barnett, USA

Parque de Obras Publicas

● *Left*

Tarifa, on the Strait of Gibraltar, is just a few long tacks from Africa. Windsurfing zealots from around the world encamp on the area's long, sandy beaches.
Photographer:
Larry C. Price, USA

● *Above*

A water bicycle built for two: Vacationers peddle across the calm Mediterranean waters off Tossa de Mar on the Costa Brava. Although conservative swimwear was required on beaches during the Franco years, topless sunning is now the norm at most Spanish resorts.
Photographer:
Mick Greenwood, Britain

● *Right*

Sunworshiping at Tossa de Mar:
The former fishing village now
has 100 hotels that host a summer invasion led by Britons,
Germans and the French. It
swells the town's population of
3,500 fivefold.
Photographer:
Mick Greenwood, Britain

● *Left*

Montse Aragonés scored high in the *Day in the Life of Spain* photo contest with this shot of a Ferris wheel under construction in Madrid.
Photography contest winner:
Montse Aragonés, Spain

● *Above*

Time capsule: Miguel Zabaleta, 59, at his farm in Leiza in northern Spain. Photographer Michael O'Brien says of his assignment, "Nothing I did was modern. Thirty or 40 years ago you would have gotten the same shots. Here, life hasn't changed much."
Photographer:
Michael O'Brien, USA

Left

chool bussing: Verónica Bereira nd Indara Etxebarría, students a Bermeo convent school, how *Day in the Life* photogra- her Andy Levin what good iends they are.
hotographer:
ndy Levin, USA

● *Left*

Retired construction worker Antonio Vizcarro and his wife, Elvira, stand in the doorway of their home, a former fisherman's cottage in Peñíscola, a Mediter- ranean resort north of Valencia.
Photographer:
Patrick Tehan, USA

● *Left*

Homestead: This *cortijo,* or
farmhouse, in the province of
Sevilla is patterned after the old
Roman villas of Spain. A well-
equipped *cortijo* has its own flour
mill, olive press and winery, as
well as a variety of livestock.
Photographer:
Koldo Chamorro, Spain

● *Above*

Homework: María López studies
in the kitchen of her family's
farmhouse in Castilla-León. Her
father, the mayor of Itero de la
Vega (pop. 308), grows alfalfa
and sugar beets.
Photographer:
Pedro Coll, Spain

● *Above*

Juan Antonio Fernández presses a 154-pound barbell as Mari-Carmen Arillo lends a hand. Like many Spaniards, Fernández is a fitness fanatic. "This helps me relax after a hard day at the factory," he says.
Photographer:
Peter Turnley, USA

● *Right*

Two-year-old Musa watches his father, Abdul Sattar Khan, hang a picture of himself on the wall of his study. An imam, or Moslem religious leader, the 40-year-old Pakistani heads Ahmadia Mission of Islam, the first mosque built in Spain since Ferdinand and Isabella drove the Moors from the Iberian peninsula in 1492. The mosque, which draws about 100 of the faithful, is located in Pedro Abad, near the 15th-century Moslem stronghold of Córdoba. Of his 10 years in Spain the imam says, "I have found the people here to be more open than any others in Europe."
Photographer:
Tomasz Tomaszewski, Poland

● *Left*

Since 1419, Dominican nuns at Las Dueñas convent have paced this quiet balcony in the shadow of Salamanca's cathedral. The community of 38 now makes ends meet by selling homemade candy to tourists.
Photographer:
Barry Lewis, Britain

● *Above*

Cypress trees catch the afternoon light at the municipal cemetery in the walled medieval village of Morella, in eastern Spain.
Photographer:
Patrick Tehan, USA

● *Above*

Though he kept his composure long enough to become the *Day in the Life of Spain* cover boy, Diego, three, has definitely had enough. His mother, strawberry picker Dominga Montado, 22, dressed him in a *traje corto,* an Andalusian cowboy outfit, complete with boots and chaps, for the fiesta in their village of La Puebla de Guzmán.
Photographer:
Cristina García Rodero, Spain

● *Right*

Shepherd Francisco "Patxi" Barriola, 57, with his daughter, María José, two, in their family home in Leiza, Navarra. American photographer Michael O'Brien was struck by "the contrast between this rugged man and his tender, beautiful daughter. He works outside, and his skin is dark. She has the skin of an angel."
Photographer:
Michael O'Brien, USA

● *Left*

Dancer Isabel Triviño, 19, stands
in the entrance hall of a flamenco
school in Madrid. "I've wanted
to be a professional flamenco
dancer all my life," says Triviño,
who travels from Madrid's
western suburbs to attend four
to five hours of classes daily.
Tuition is steep, and she must
teach popular dance to pay for
her instruction.
Photographer:
Eddie Adams, USA

● *Above*

The string section of Spain's
National Orchestra rehearses in
Madrid's Teatro Real for its
3,000th concert. The govern-
ment-financed symphony orchestra was created in 1940 and
includes 120 musicians and an
equal number of vocalists.
Photographer:
Rick Smolan, USA

It is as ritualized as a coronation and more visceral than a boxing match: the bull, the matador and the crowd, the trinity of the *corrida de toros*. The matador's "suit of lights" glitters while the hooves pound the arena. The crowd roars, "¡*Ole!*" to the dance-like feints of the matador. White handkerchiefs flutter as the *toro,* or bull, goes down and blood spills on the sand.

Passionate hordes flock to the bullring. Young men grow riotous with the running of the bulls. Boys dream of becoming *toreros,* or matadors. More than a sport, the *corrida de toros* is a fiesta of glory and ritual, of glamour and blood.

Bullfighting is big business, employing 20,000 Spaniards. Thirty-two million spectators witness the deaths of some 25,000 bulls each year. Matadors who reach the top and stay there become living legends. The half-dozen superstars of the sport earn a million dollars per year.

There is an old Spanish adage: The horn-wounds of ambition are the worst of all. Only a handful of the young men who begin the grueling *torero* apprenticeship will make it into the great rings. But technique is only a relative asset anyway. Every *aficionado* knows that matadors are not made— a matador is born, ready for the bull.

● *Left*

At Madrid's bullfighting school, Alvaro González trains against an iron bull. This is the final act of the fight, when the matador lunges over the horns to sink the sword between the bull's shoulders. Alvaro will soon face year-old bulls and may someday share the ring with 1,300-pound four-year-olds.
Photographer:
Mark S. Wexler, USA

● *Above*

Manuel Martínez, director of the matador school, shows students how to approach the bull. "I don't accept any kid unless he attends a normal school as well," says Martínez, who opened the training facility in Madrid's Casa de Campo Park 12 years ago. "If they only came here, the kids would become punch-drunk on the bull."
Photographer:
Mark S. Wexler, USA

● *Above*

Test of courage: Valencia University students taunt a year-old bull during a local fiesta.
Photography contest winner:
Alejandro Ribera, Spain

● *Following pages 170-171*

A Spanish legend: Retired matador Antonio Ordóñez in the bullring of his hometown of Ronda. Considered by many (including his American friends Ernest Hemingway and Orson Welles) to be the greatest of all postwar bullfighters, Ordóñez began his career in 1951 at age 19 and retired, still at the top, in 1981. On May 7, 1987, Welles, according to his wishes, was buried at the bullfighter's ranch in southern Andalucía.

Photographer:
David Hume Kennerly, USA

● *Right*

The *traje corto,* or short suit, is the Andalusian's traditional riding gear. It provides the freedom of movement necessary for the equestrian. Joaquín Moreno de Silva, one of Spain's top *rejoneadores* (the master horsemen who fight the bull from the saddle), wears the *traje* while testing a calf at his father's ranch in Palma del Río.
Photographer:
Jodi Cobb, USA

● *Right*

A Madrid *punky* pins a new button on his friend under the colonnades of the 17th-century Plaza Mayor. Although the *punkies* do not care much for foreign tourists, New York photographer Maddy Miller was able to spend May 7th with several (Animal, Makoka, Monster and May) who live in the plaza and sleep in the parking garages beneath the ancient square: "I spent the whole day with them. We had no common language, but we slowly built a rapport. They took me everywhere. I gave them some money and told them to get something to eat. Instead, they took me to lunch with the money."
Photographer:
Maddy Miller, USA

● *Above*

Who's next?: At a wedding party in a Madrid park, members of Spain's young and fashionable set are discussing love and marriage.
Photographer:
Rick Smolan, USA

● *Right*

Young love in Vitoria, the capital of the Basque country: During Franco's day, public displays of affection could lead to arrest, but now Spanish plazas are filled with kissing couples.
Photographer:
Robin Moyer, USA

● Left

n guard: A shepherd and his
heepdog watch over their flock
a field near Haro in La Rioja
egion.
hotographer:
ndrew Stawicki, Canada

● Above

Swimming class at Barcelona's
La Salle Bonanova sports center: Eight-year-old Nicolás
Pascual Equisvany snapped this
contest winner with a Kodak
camera given to him by veteran
photographer Mary Ellen Mark.
*Children's photography contest
winner:*
**Nicolás Pascual Equisvany,
Spain**

● Following pages 178-179

A long day of tilling ends for
Antonio Machuca, his son Rafael
and a nephew in Marinaleda.
Machuca is one of a small number of Andalusian farmers still
using the horse-drawn, hand-held
Roman plow. He is also one of
the few agricultural workers in
Marinaleda who own land. Most
of the town's 2,380 inhabitants
are landless laborers who find
employment only two months a
year on the *latifundios*—large,
private estates that surround
the town.
Photographer:
Koldo Chamorro, Spain

● Following pages 180-181

Weekend cottage: The
18th-century Royal Palace of
Aranjuez, on the banks of the
Tajo River, 30 miles south of
Madrid. Originally a summer
home for the Bourbon kings, it
now hosts visiting heads of state.
Photographer:
Georg Gerster, Switzerland

● Following pages 182-183

During the Moslem holy days
of Ramadan, members of the
Abdesalam family must wait until
sundown to eat. "The women
were extremely shy and left the
room when I came in", said French
photographer Jean-Pierre Laffont.
Photographer:
Jean-Pierre Laffont, France

Koldo Chamorro

Jean-Pierre Laffont

Fourteen-year-olds Laina
González, Arantxa Hernández,
Marina Aragonés and Yolanda
Cortés are at a country club
wedding reception near Madrid.
Photographer:
Rick Smolan, USA

● *Above*

At the same reception are men-about-town José María Causín, Valentín González, Javier Fernández and Gonzalo Gilsanz.
Photographer:
Rick Smolan, USA

● *Previous pages 186-187*

The Igueldo lighthouse stands guard over the Bay of Biscay in the Basque province of Guipúzcoa.
Photographer:
Dan Dry, USA

● *Left*

Duck and run: Two Barcelona boys avoid the 50-peseta (40-cent) subway fare. "I was checking my light meter when I suddenly saw this rapid movement," says amateur photographer Gerónimo Mota, "I turned and shot." Mota is used to catching quick action on film. He's a cameraman for a local television station.

Photography contest winner:
Gerónimo Mota, Spain

● *Above*

A signalman gives the green light to a train pulling into Barcelona's Plaza de Cataluña station. Some 50,000 Spaniards commute into the city daily.

Photographer:
Daniel Lainé, France

● *Previous pages 190-191*

A helicopter view of Ares del Maestre, 4,000 feet above sea level in the Alto Maestrazgo mountain range in Castellón province. A nearly impregnable fortress, the cliff town was the last spot in eastern Spain to fall to Christian forces during the reconquest of the Moorish invaders. When the defenders surrendered to Valencian King James I in 1233, every man, woman and child was slaughtered.
Photographer:
Patrick Tehan, USA

● *Left*

Dusk falls on a side street in the Andalusian town of Ronda.
Photographer:
David Hume Kennerly, USA

● *Above*

At a Benedictine convent near Madrid, Sister Nieves reads her breviary before retiring.
Photographer:
Anne Day, USA

● *Previous pages 194-195*

Chicago-born model Shell Neal, 25, applies makeup at a fashion show in Tarrasa, near Barcelona, the center of Cataluña's textile industry. Neal moved from Paris to Barcelona a year ago to join the growing number of international models on the Spanish fashion circuit. "Fashion in Spain is really on the way up," says Neal, who also appreciates Barcelona's low cost of living.
Photographer:
George Steinmetz, USA

● *Below*

Models Carmen Tassani (left) and María Luisa Parera are about to strut down the runway at the Tarrasa fashion show. Spanish fashion is on the rise with the emergence of a group of internationally acclaimed designers, including Adolfo Domínguez, Purificación García and Roberto Verinno.
Photographer:
George Steinmetz, USA

● *Above, top*

A lot on her mind: The toast of Madrid's "la Movida" youth culture, singer Martirio (Martyrdom) describes herself as a "mixture of the old and the new, the beautiful and the bizarre." Born in the southern provincial town of Huelva, 33-year-old Martirio, whose real name is María Isabel Quiñones Martínez, mixes traditional Spanish styles with modern international punk and sings her own strident rock lyrics to the clatter of castanets. "People see me as their mother and their girlfriend," says Martirio. "They applaud me because I am a reflection of their own psyches."
Photographer:
Nicole Bengiveno, USA

● *Above*

This well-dressed Spanish *punky* wears live rodents and lives in an abandoned Barcelona building with 10 others. "Most of them are runaways," says photographer Mary Ellen Mark, "and when I asked them if they had a message for the public, they said, 'There's no future.' That's the same message I got from runaways in the States."
Photographer:
Mary Ellen Mark, USA

● *Left*

Sweet dreams: When Alvaro González goes to sleep, he may well dream about the day he becomes a top matador billed on real posters.
Photographer:
Mark S. Wexler, USA

● *Above*

Cellist Yvonne Timoianu and pianist Alexandru Preda perform in one of Ronda's old palaces.
Photographer:
David Hume Kennerly, USA

● *Left*

Regulars at Sevilla's La Garrocha
bar whirl and stamp their way
through a *sevillana,* an intricate
but very popular folk dance that
literally means "from Sevilla."
The *sevillana* is accompanied by
guitars, hand-clapping and singing, and hundreds of schools
have sprung up to teach the
dance to Spaniards and tourists
alike. *Newsweek* photographer
Peter Turnley left his heart in
Sevilla: "I can't remember a city
where so many people were
happy about the place they live.
It wasn't pride or chauvinism.
They genuinely think they live in
a great place. And they're right."
Photographer:
Peter Turnley, USA

● *Above*

A crowd pleaser: Fans show
their enthusiasm for singer
Alejandro Abad at Barcelona's
Area disco.
Photographer:
Sigfrid Casals, Spain

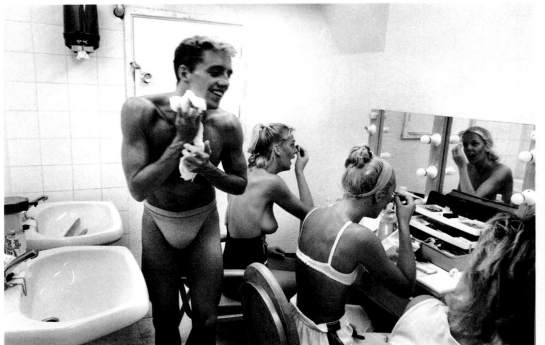

● *Above*

Dancers share a dressing-room joke after the last act at La Scala nightclub in the Gran Canaria resort of Playa de San Agustín. Scotsman Gary Breslin and fellow Britons Geraldine Webb and Melanie Smith belong to a 30-member dance troupe that performs Las Vegas-style variety shows. The company also includes Americans, South Africans and Spaniards.

Photographer:
Arthur Grace, USA

● *Right*

Break a wing: Performers wish each other luck on an opening night at Barcelona's El Molino music hall. The sex-oriented variety-show theater has been a local institution for over 80 years. More than in any other Spanish city, Barcelona's nightlife caters to the bizarre, with a wide range of sex shows, topless bars and transvestite clubs.

Photographer:
Mary Ellen Mark, USA

● *Above*

Closing time at a Barcelona café, and the waiter waits for the last guest, *Day in the Life* photographer Seny Norasingh, to depart.
Photographer:
Seny Norasingh, USA

● *Right*

Place your bets: The roulette wheel is about to take a spin at the elegant Taoro Casino on Tenerife in the Canary Islands. Photographer Daniel Aubry had a dicey experience at the Taoro: "I set my lights up the day before the shoot, and when I arrived to take the pictures everything was perfect. The table was crowded, and I had two and a half hours to go before the end of May 7th. Then the lights went out. It was a power failure. They didn't come back on until half an hour before midnight." As luck would have it, Aubry got his picture with minutes to spare.
Photographer:
Daniel Aubry, USA

● *Following pages 206-207*

As May 7th came to a close, Basque photographer Angel Ruiz de Azúa captured the city of Madrid from the 725-foot Tower of Spain. The tower was built to transmit Spanish television across the peninsula during the 1982 World Cup soccer championships.
Photographer:
Angel Ruiz de Azúa, Spain

Neal Slavin

Photographers' Assignment Locations

El Ferrol/2

Pancar de Llanes/28

Sama de Langreo/29 · Treceño/87

Bermeo/5

Portugalete/33
· Guernica/
Bilbao/46, 100
· Ceánuri/8
Mondragón/

Sobrado de los Monjes/79

Santiago de Compostela/14, 43

Piornedo/99

Riaño/95

Vitoria/6

La Estrada/77

Haro/89

Orense/50

Burgos/97

Vigo/54

Itero de la Vega/19

Valladolid/61

P.F. Bentley

A seasoned bullfighter gets fitted
into a new "suit of lights" at a
Madrid tailor.

Salamanca/56

Guadalajara/40

Barajas/21, 73

★ Madrid/1, 8, 9, 10, 11, 17, 34, 35,
57, 65, 82, 85, 102

Coria/38

Getafe/26

Toledo/45, 62, 88

Trujillo/81

Campo de Criptan

Herrera de la Mancha/4

Almagro/32

Gerd Ludwig

Whistling as he works, a Gomeran shepherd
communicates over hill and valley.

Córdoba/94

Cazorla/53

El Cerro de Andévalo/30 · Palma del Río/18

Sevilla/69, 96

Palos de la Frontera/15 · Marinaleda/13

Guadix/64

Granada/74

Tabernas/

Jerez/39 · Ronda/47

Marbella/48

Cádiz/86

Barbate/41 · La Línea de la Concepción/66
Algeciras/75

Lanzarote/68

Puerto de la Cruz/4

Antonio Suárez

Melilla/51

Gomera/58

Las Palmas de Gran Canaria/78

Maspalomas/37

Mini-Hollywood in Tabernas, Andalucía, the
home of many spaghetti westerns.

San Sebastián/23

Villafranca de Ordizia/31

● Leiza/71

● Pamplona/60

● Campo/22

● Figueras/25

● Vich/3

● Zaragoza/24, 44, 98

● San Sadurní de Noya/12

● Barcelona/7, 16, 52, 59, 70, 83, 91, 104

● Belchite/101

Cuenca/27

● Mahón/20

Frank Fournier

Folk dancers celebrate the opening of a new public park in the Madrid suburb of Getafe.

● Valldemosa/72

Kaku Kurita

Top fashion designer Adolfo Domínguez heads for his workshop in Orense, Galicia.

● Valencia/5, 93

● Almusafes/90

● Ibiza/76

● Denia/49

● Archena/36

● Murcia/103

Al Satterwhite

Basque farmwoman Ciriaca Eloroza near the town of Mondragón.

1 Eddie Adams
2 José María Alguersuari
3 Carlos de Andrés
4 Daniel Aubry
5 Eric Lars Bakke
6 James Balog
7 Nina Barnett
8 Letizia Battaglia
9 Nicole Bengiveno
10 P.F. Bentley
11 Miguel Bergasa
12 Sigfrid Casals
13 Koldo Chamorro
14 Aaron Chang
15 Gary S. Chapman
16 Paul Chesley
17 Rich Clarkson
18 Jodi Cobb
19 Pedro Coll
20 J.D. Dallet
21 Anne Day
22 Jay Dickman
23 Dan Dry
24 Misha Erwitt
25 Gerrit Fokkema
26 Frank Fournier
27 Raphaël Gaillarde
28 Germán Gallego
29 Sam Garcia
30 Cristina García Rodero
31 Jerry Gay
32 Georg Gerster
33 Diego Goldberg
34 Lynn Goldsmith
35 Felipe González

36 Miguel González
37 Arthur Grace
38 Skeeter Hagler
39 Dirck Halstead
40 Manuel Hernández de León
41 Fernando Herráez
42 Ethan Hoffman
43 Graciela Iturbide
44 Frank Johnston
45 H.M. don Juan Carlos
46 Robb Kendrick
47 David Hume Kennerly
48 Douglas Kirkland
49 Steve Krongard
50 Kaku Kurita
51 Jean-Pierre Laffont
52 Daniel Lainé
53 Frans Lanting
54 Sarah Leen
55 Andy Levin
56 Barry Lewis
57 John Loengard
58 Gerd Ludwig
59 Mary Ellen Mark
60 Stephanie Maze
61 Wally McNamee
62 Dilip Mehta
63 Doug Menuez
64 Claus C. Meyer
65 Maddy Miller
66 Carlos Monge
67 Robin Moyer
68 Carlos Navajas
69 Matthew Naythons
70 Seny Norasingh
71 Michael O'Brien
72 Graeme Outerbridge
73 Bernardo Pérez
74 Bill Pierce
75 Larry C. Price
76 Roger Ressmeyer

77 Jim Richardson
78 Juantxu Rodríguez
79 Benito Román
80 Galen Rowell
81 Robert Royal
82 Angel Ruiz de Azúa
83 Sebastião Salgado
84 Al Satterwhite
85 Alberto Schommer
86 Marta Sentís
87 Neal Slavin
88 Rick Smolan
89 Andrew Stawicki
90 Víctor Steinberg
91 George Steinmetz
92 Antonio Suárez
93 Patrick Tehan
94 Tomasz Tomaszewski
95 David C. Turnley
96 Peter Turnley
97 Neal Ulevich
98 Jerry Valente
99 John Vink
100 Wendy Watriss
101 David H. Wells
102 Mark S. Wexler
103 Arnaud de Wildenberg
104 Ramón Zabalza

A Day in the Life of Spain Revisited

Basilio Perona Cortés

Brazilian photographer Sebastião Salgado encounters an impromptu flamenco dance in San Adrián de Besos, Barcelona.

Rick Smolan

Right angle: Neal Slavin and Pierre de Oliveira Castro arrange some of the world's best photographers for the group portrait.

W hen members of the advance staff for *A Day in the Life of Spain* (DITLOS) first visited Madrid in January 1987, they immediately impressed the cool, laid-back Spaniards as a typical bunch of mad, impetuous Americans. Their idea probably sounded as implausible as Christopher Columbus's pitch to Ferdinand and Isabella 500 years earlier. The DITLOS team offered to assemble a multinational staff of dozens in Madrid and find a team of crack assignment editors who would be sent throughout Spain in search of photographic subjects. Simultaneously, it would track down 100 of the world's best photojournalists and persuade them to come to Spain to shoot a portrait of the entire nation in a single day. Finally, an international group of picture editors would distill the resulting 100,000 or so photographs into a high-quality coffee-table book. The *Day in the Life* folk somehow thought they could accomplish all this in 20 weeks in a country known for its beauty, culture, erudition, passion, food—just about anything but speed.

"You will die trying to do this," one Spanish journalist joked, "and I will be there to photograph it." As events unfolded, she came very close to taking that shot.

There may never be a more timely subject for a *Day in the Life* project than Spain. In little more than a decade, Spain has emerged from 40 years of virtual isolation and entered the 20th century with a vengeance. Not long ago, to stroll through Retiro, Madrid's stately central park, was to enter a time warp. Solemn-faced men and women walked along in dark Sunday suits and lace-trimmed dresses. Even small children wore business

suits and somber frocks. Today, the same park is a riot of T-shirts and track shoes, couples embracing and children frolicking. Only a dozen years ago, political discussion was rigidly controlled. Today, the cafés of Spain resound with spirited discourse on politics, art and poetry. Graffiti writers spray their political views on walls in every city and village. As the pictures in this book testify, Spain today is a vibrant and photogenic collage of old and new. "More than any other country in Europe, Spain has changed dramatically for the better in the last 10 years," says project co-director David Cohen. "It's prospering, it's blossoming—the country has gone through terrific convulsions and emerged reborn."

The *Day in the Life* team members are experts at creating their own convulsions on an international scale. Back in 1981, photographer Rick Smolan invented a new kind of photojournalistic enterprise when he persuaded 100 of the world's top photographers to join him in documenting *A Day in the Life of Australia.* No publisher Down Under would touch the idea, but no worries, mate. Aided by David Cohen—then the managing editor of Contact, the New York photo agency—Smolan and a group of friends published the book themselves, and set an antipodean record by selling 200,000 copies. *Day in the Life* books on Japan and Canada soon followed, under the imprint of Collins, a British publisher, which established an American branch and made Cohen its president. Then, in 1986, lightning struck in the form of *A Day in the Life of America,* which spent the better part of a year on *The New York Times* best-seller list and sold nearly a million copies in the process. With that kind of track record, *A Day in the Life of Spain* must have been a snap, right?

Try telling that to the hundreds of people who sweated *sangre* to make it happen.

Every time we start one of these projects, it's a little like jumping off a cliff and hoping the parachute opens on the way down," says project co-director Smolan. "Things always go wrong, and even though we've been through five *Day in the Life* projects, each has its own twists and turns. In short, we're never quite sure it's going to work." As usual, the DITLOS staff began this project in a free-fall. Only a few months before shoot day, the photographers weren't yet lined up and the sponsorship wasn't arranged—and, of course, nobody could tell if the book would capture the spirit of Spain until the film was on the light table. This time around, though, the *Day in the Life* crew had a powerful—and powerfully competent—ally in its corner. "If you want to know why we decided to make a book about Spain," says Cohen, "I can give you a two-word answer—Ignacio Vasallo. He's one of the most capable and dynamic men we've met on any of our projects."

Search and deploy: The DITLOS assignment editing team. (Standing) regional editors Mark Potok, Devyani Kamdar, Dominique Mollard, Karen Polk, Susan Linnée and David Baird; (seated) chief writer Tom Burns, associate managing editor Amy Janello and managing editor Brennon Jones. Regional editors Isabel Soto and Anthony Luke were off on assignment.

Rick Smolan

The eyes have had it: The DITLOS photo editors and design team looked at 120,000 images. (Standing) Steve Ettlinger, designer Jim Stockton, Mark Grosset and Don Abood; (seated) Mary Dawn Earley, art director Tom Walker, Alfonso Gutiérrez and Jordi Socias.

Rick Smolan

In 1986, when *A Day in the Life of America* was being produced, Vasallo, the hyperactive head of Spanish tourism, visited the *Day in the Life* command center in Denver with Daniel Aubry, a long-time friend and one of the 200 photojournalists on the America shoot. "We were surprised. We were expecting a tourism guy in a suit, and Ignacio turned up wearing jeans like us," recalls Smolan. Vasallo said that he wanted the *Day in the Life* team to come work its magic in his country. "At that time," DITLOS general manager Cathy Quealy remembers, "we had countries lining up at our door. We were even invited to produce *A Day in the Life of the World* by a United Nations agency." The *Day in the Life* team members heard out Vasallo's proposal, and his obvious enthusiasm for his homeland won them over. So did Aubry's assurances that "if Vasallo says it's a go project, it's a go project." Another meeting was scheduled and then another. By the fourth get-together, in December 1986, New York staffers had begun studying Spanish and were booking flights for a January trip to Madrid to meet potential sponsors assembled by Vasallo.

That trip clinched the project. "Ignacio had done all the preliminary work for us," Quealy recounts. "He opened all the doors."

The *Day in the Life* projects do not accept government money as a matter of principle, to avoid editorial interference. As a matter of practicality, however, all *Day in the Life* books require sponsorship from a consortium of public-spirited companies that agree, at the outset, to relinquish any editorial control over the final product that will bear their name. The shooting budget for *A Day in the Life of Spain* was $1.4 million—as much as for a small feature film.

"The sponsors made it all possible," says corporate relations director Miriam Hernández. Telefónica and Campsa, the Spanish telephone and oil companies, and McDonnell Douglas fueled the project with cash. Iberia flew the staff and photographers to Madrid from points as diverse as Tokyo, Los Angeles, New Delhi and Rome. Avis cars and RENFE trains transported the photographers around the country, where Sol Hotels and National Paradors provided accommodations. Madrid's stately Palace Hotel housed the raffish DITLOS team in the capital, and Kodak provided the photographers with film, processing and technical support—as well as the brightly colored bags that quickly became status symbols. Apple Computer came through with Macintoshes for the photographers and lent the DITLOS staff computers to help with the project's information needs, including logistics and assignments for 100 demanding photojournalists.

Even the computers, though, couldn't calculate what happened in late January. The good news was that after four years of negotiating to do *A Day in the Life of the Soviet Union,* permission was suddenly granted. The bad news was that the Soviets wanted the book published in time for the 70th anniversary of the Russian Revolution, in November 1987—less than 10 months away.

Wallflowers: (Standing) Frank Fournier, Spanish tourism director Ignacio Vasallo, Carlos Vasallo, Rick Pappas, Claus Meyer; (seated) Doug Kirkland, Devi Kamdar and project co-director David Cohen.

High roller: Bermudian photographer Graeme Outerbridge hangs from atop a schooner's mast in the harbor of Palma de Mallorca.

"There was much agonizing," Quealy remembers. "The people in Spain had been so wonderful, and we were all geared up for the DITLOS project. But we just couldn't pass up a chance to do the Soviet Union." With a deep breath, the *Day in the Life* staff decided to do both books at once.

The group split into two teams. One, under Cohen, went to Moscow. The other, under Smolan, masterminded the Spain project. Because of the problems of communicating between Moscow and the outside world, all of the logistics for the Soviet team—from travel arrangements to film shipments—were handled from the Madrid office.

During the January trip, Quealy set about recruiting administrative staff—from translators to publicity assistants. Managing editor Brennon Jones and his associate, Amy Janello, hunted for Spanish assignment editors, photo editors and, most important, photographers. "In three weeks, we talked to almost everyone who worked in any kind of journalistic capacity in Spain," says Janello.

By the end of March, the DITLOS headquarters in Madrid was starting to look as if it *employed* everyone who worked in any kind of journalistic capacity in Spain. "We recruited a talented group of people with an incredible passion for Spain and an enthusiasm to show it to the rest of the world," says Jones. Veteran journalists like Isabel Soto of *The New York Times,* Dominique Mollard of the Associated Press and Anthony Luke of the national news agency EFE took leaves from their demanding jobs to be a part of DITLOS. Tom Burns, *Newsweek*'s man in Madrid, became a key player. "He was crucial to the project," Jones points out, "not only for his contribution as a writer, but for his extraordinary access and

No hay problema: The DITLOS staff can get anything done by mañana. (Standing) Rick Smolan, Rusty Conway, Cathy Quealy, Maureen Kelly, Pierre de Oliveira Castro, Miriam

Hernández, Karen Bakke, Milagros Bello; (seated) Jennifer Erwitt, Laura Lowenthal, Juan Galiano, Marie-Claire Rodríguez, Fernando de Miguel.

The King and I: In the royal hobby room, King Juan Carlos and *Day in the Life of Spain* co-director Rick Smolan talk computers.

On a roll: Daniel Aubry prepares to turn in his film.

Black-and-white decision: The photo editors look for prints.

Booking passage: Travel director Karen Bakke, undeterred by Spanish strikes and slow-downs, kept the DITLOS photographers up in the air.

contacts. He knows *everybody* in Spain. If he couldn't solve a problem, he always knew who could."

Everybody in Spain seemed ecstatic about the project. King Juan Carlos agreed not only to be photographed for the book, but to be one of the photographers. (He was later joined by Spanish Prime Minister Felipe González, a fellow photo buff.) On a few occasions, the king summoned Rick Smolan to Zarzuela Palace to discuss their shared passions—computers and photography.

By late March, only six weeks before the photographers were due to arrive, the assignment editors fanned out across Spain, scouting locations, arranging contacts and, hardest of all in a society that values its privacy, finding families who were willing to put up photographers in their houses. The editors came back full of ideas—and full of stories. Karen Polk, for instance, found herself enchanted by the northwest region of Galicia. One day, she was driving through a heavy fog when her car crested a hill: "Suddenly, there was a herd of wild horses in front of me, and the sun cut through the clouds. There were these emerald fields and black cliffs plunging down to the ocean. It was magnificent. I wished one of the photographers were there with me at that moment." She drove to the village at the base of the hill and met a local camera store dealer who had heard about the project through a mailing from Kodak. Shyly, he offered to host a photographer on shoot day. When Polk turned to leave, he stopped her, saying, "Remember, even if I never see you again, you'll always have a friend here."

Meanwhile, back in Madrid the DITLOS office combined the frenzy of an election campaign headquarters and the high-tech calm of Mission Control as dozens of bodies hunched over the bluish glow of computer screens. Publicity director Maureen Kelly and her assistant, Pierre de Oliveira Castro, put 900 press kits together to inform media throughout Spain of the project. When they went to Madrid's main post office to mail the kits, they confronted a publicist's nightmare—an obscure regulation that allowed no more than 100 pieces of mail to be sent by one organization from the post office on the same day. "We went back for nine days, but we finally got them out," Kelly recalls. And it was worth the effort. By May 7th, *A Day in the Life of Spain* was a national event, followed by every Spaniard who glanced at a newspaper, tuned in to a radio station or watched the evening news.

DITLOS had a built-in safety valve against the pressures of tight deadlines and clerical snafus. "I figured out pretty quickly that in Spain when someone commits to do something by a certain date, that is only a rough estimate," says Cathy Quealy, a veteran of *Day in the Life* projects. "But our deadline was firm. That's why we had a staff that was willing to work 18 hours a day. And they usually did!" The heart of that staff was a young, multi-lingual, multinational group—including Rusty Conway, Juan Galiano, Laura Lowenthal, Fernando de Miguel and Marie-Claire Rodríquez—that melted cultural differences, kept copy machines and messengers moving and

Veteran *Day in the Life*r Jennifer Erwitt shows Laura Lowenthal the ropes on an Apple computer.

General manager Cathy Quealy manages the impossible.

amicably interpreted everything from Spanish newspaper articles to the latest pop music for their DITLOS compatriots. And for special problems, DITLOS relied on the remarkable talents of Aurora Núñez, the tourist board's premier troubleshooter, who was on 24-hour call.

All 100 photographers descended on Madrid five days before May 7th, right on schedule, thanks to the wizardry of travel director Karen Bakke. Canadian photographer Dilip Mehta found himself trapped in Delhi by an early monsoon. Bakke routed him through London. *Time* magazine's Robin Moyer needed Bakke's help in connecting flights from Hong Kong via Tokyo. A handful of DITLOS photographers were trapped in Miami. Bakke got them on a last-minute flight to New York and then on to Madrid. Back home now in Denver, she talks about those nail-biting days almost as if they were fun.

And, for a lot of people, they *were* fun. For 100 kids who participated in a Kodak-sponsored camera clinic in Retiro Park, the DITLOS project meant a chance to learn how to take pictures from the world's best photographers. The professionals gave away another 100 free Kodak cameras on shoot day. These 200 children snapped some of the shots you see on pages 100-101 of this book.

For many of the photographers, DITLOS was like an annual convention. The global tribe of photojournalists with camera bags toted across seven continents filled the spacious, elegant lobby of the Palace Hotel. Their talk was of old friends and wars, shared anxieties and exhaustions and fleeting moments of triumph. But they also came to pursue their craft. Out of hundreds of photojournalists longing to be on the project, only the very best were chosen. By dawn on May 7, 1987, these professionals were revved-up and ready to go.

For some of the photographers the day would test their patience as much as their skills. American surfing photographer Aaron Chang's primary assignment ended early, when he was ejected from a cathedral after the priests discovered that *Day in the Life* books occasionally contained pictures of nude women. Dilip Mehta was confronted briefly by irate Toledans who thought that the arrival of the king's helicopter entourage, which Mehta was photographing from the ground, might be some sort of assault on the medieval city. Six-foot-two-inch Sam Garcia had the challenge of his career squeezing himself into the mine shafts of Asturias. "Those were the worst possible conditions I have ever photographed. I can't imagine anyone doing it more than once, let alone every day for 34 years like one miner I met," recalls the New York photographer. And Swiss aerial photographer Georg Gerster was grounded when red tape kept him from flying with the Spanish Air Force. Quick work by Tom Burns and Brennon Jones, and financial aid from Kodak, got him aloft in a private plane.

But such disappointments were few, and most of the photographers returned to Madrid on May 8th with stories of the extraordinary welcome they received from the Spanish people.

Anne Day found only peace in a high-tech convent in Barajas where the nuns do computer data processing while singing Gregorian chants. *People* magazine's Maddy Miller befriended a group of punks in Madrid's Plaza Mayor, and they took her to lunch at a soup kitchen. Madrileña Cristina García Rodero, totally lost in the dead of night in Huelva province, was rescued by the local Guardia Civil, whose members escorted her to the door of the rural house where she was to spend the night.

Dan Dry was worried about shooting in a country where he didn't know the language. "I was your basic stupid American," he says. Then he discovered that eight of the 11 children in his host family had studied English in the United States. "On May 7th, I had eight different guides and interpreters," says the Kentuckian.

The photographers regrouped in Madrid with more than stories. They brought back 3,000 rolls of exposed film, 120,000 images in all, that had to be inventoried, processed, catalogued and edited. "What we were doing was more akin to filmmaking than producing a book," Smolan reflects. "One team after another passed the

Corporate roundtable: A weekly meeting of DITLOS project sponsors.

(photo credit: Rick Smolan)

torch on to the group after it. Each one burned itself out and handed it on to the next group."

The photo editors, led by Mary Dawn Earley, took those words almost too literally. Working day and night, they whittled down the photographs to only 500 in barely a week. "It was grueling but fun," Earley recalls. "There was the excitement of not knowing what images you were about to edit and the enjoyment of working as a team." Picture editors, like photographers, seldom have the chance to work together.

The photograph on the cover of this book, by Spanish photojournalist Cristina García Rodero, was suggested by Madrid picture editor Jordi Socias. The mother and child seem to symbolize Spain to foreign eyes. But Socias was even fonder of the photograph that appears on page 162, in which the boy's calm has dissolved into tears. He said it would show that Spaniards know how to laugh at themselves.

Once editing was completed, all 120,000 images landed on the desk of logistics director Jennifer Erwitt, who inexplicably remained calm while trafficking this mountain of film. The 500 photos selected by the editors for the book were now ready for members of the editorial team, who would research and write captions, and for the design board of art director Tom Walker and designer Jim Stockton.

"Before you start, you have an idea of what the book will look like," Walker says. "But it never turns out that way." He and his staff set to work trying to create a book that would carry the reader through the course of a Spanish day. "Photographers don't always keep careful notes," he says, "and it was important that the time sequence be right." While designing DITLOS, Walker and his team were also working on *A Day in the Life of the Soviet Union,* which was shot only one week after the Spanish extravaganza. "It wasn't as difficult as I thought, turning out both books. But time was tight, and there was no room for screw-ups." Walker's worst nightmare was that he might get the two books confused. Happily, there are no layouts of flamenco dancers in Siberia or the Soviet army marching on Sevilla.

The book you hold is the result of risks: the gamble of the photojournalist who traded a lucrative assignment for a week of his time, little money and no guarantee he would get a picture in the volume; the risk the sponsors assumed when they lent their trademarks and parted with their cash for something over which they had no control; the risk that the office staff, editorial team and design crew would go completely mad as they tried to create a perfect product in too few months. And, as seems to happen at the end of each of these projects, staff members are now almost evenly split. Half of them are just about ready to plunge into a new one. The other half are vowing, to anybody who will listen, that they'll never do it again.

Maybe they mean it; maybe they don't. But there is a good chance that mañana will bring another *Day.*

—Michael Ryan

Photographers' Biographies

A Day in the Life of Australia 1981

Eddie Adams
American/New York, New York
Winner of the Pulitzer Prize and the Silver Grand Prix Award of the Advertising Association of Japan, Adams is one of the most decorated and published photographers in the United States, with more than 500 awards to his credit. He has photographed leaders in all fields, from heads of state to superstars of film, sports and high fashion.

José María Alguersuari
Spanish/Barcelona
Alguersuari is a photographer for *La Vanguardia,* Barcelona's largest daily newspaper. His work has also appeared in *El Periódico, Match, Interviú, Mondial* and *Expression.* He is associated with the Spanish photo agency AGE FotoStock.

Daniel Aubry
American/New York, New York
Aubry maintains a mix of editorial, corporate and advertising clients as well as undertaking fine-art photography projects. He has photographed two tourism campaigns for the Spanish government and routinely works for both *Connoisseur* and *Travel & Leisure* magazines. Aubry has won two creativity awards from *Art Direction* magazine for best editorial photography.

Denver, Colorado 1984

Eric Lars Bakke
American/Denver, Colorado
Bakke is co-owner of a Denver-based photographers' group called Photostaff Inc. In the 1985 Pictures of the Year competition, sponsored by the National Press Photographers Association and held at the University of Missouri School of Journalism, he was awarded an honorable mention for a news picture story. He also won *Sporting News* magazine's prize for best sports picture in 1984 and 1985. Suburban Newspapers of America awarded him first place in feature photography in 1977. Bakke is a former chief photographer for *The Denver Post.*

James Balog
American/Boulder, Colorado
Balog won the 1987 World Press Photo competition for nature and landscape photography, as well as several awards in the 1987 Pictures of the Year contest. He is a frequent contributor to *National Geographic, Smithsonian* and Time-Life publications. The International Center of Photography, in New York, recently published Balog's first book, *Wildlife Requiem.* His work has been exhibited widely in American art galleries and museums.

Nina Barnett
American/New York, New York
Barnett is a freelance photographer whose work has been published in *Fortune, Forbes, Money* and *The New York Times Magazine.* A former art production editor, Barnett was a photographer for *A Day in the Life of America.*

Letizia Battaglia
Italian/Palermo
Battaglia is the publisher of *Fotografia,* a photographic magazine for women, and *Grandevu,* a monthly magazine of photography, politics and culture. She also heads La Luna, a publisher of literature and sociological and anthropological works, and is the artistic director of a gallery and school of photography in Palermo. Battaglia was previously a staff photographer for *L'Ora.* In 1985, she won the prestigious W. Eugene Smith grant to continue a photographic project documenting the Mafia in Sicily.

Nicole Bengiveno
American/New York, New York
Bengiveno is a staff photographer at New York's *Daily News.* She previously worked for *The San Francisco Examiner* and was named Bay Area Photographer of the Year in 1979. In 1984, she won first place in the Associated Press sports photo contest. In 1985, she was a finalist for the W. Eugene Smith grant for her work on the AIDS epidemic.

P.F. Bentley
American/San Francisco, California
P.F. Bentley is a contract photographer for *Time* magazine. In 1986, he won the Leica Medal of Excellence in Photojournalism for the western United States. For his coverage of the 1984 American presidential campaign, he won first and second place in the Pictures of the Year competition. Originally from Hawaii, he now resides in San Francisco.

Itá, Paraguay 1986

Miguel Bergasa
Spanish/Pamplona
Bergasa is a freelance photographer working in the technical division of RTVE, the Spanish television and radio network. He is co-author of the book *Fotografías.* Over the last 10 years his photographs have been shown in 25 group and 10 solo exhibitions and published in a variety of books.

Alcoy, Spain 1978

Sigfrid Casals
Spanish/Barcelona
Casals is a staff photographer for the Spanish weekly *Cambio 16* and previously worked for *El Periódico, El Noticiero Universal* and the Madrid photo agency Cover. He is co-author of the books *Nens, No Ninots* and *1981.* He received Fotopres awards in 1984 and 1985, and has exhibited at the Fotopres Gallery and at the Foreign Press Club in Madrid.

Koldo Chamorro
Spanish/Pamplona
Chamorro works for *El País* and Spanish *GEO.* He was a finalist for the W. Eugene Smith grant, received a scholarship from Dotación de Arte Castellblanch in Spain and was granted the National Institute of the Spanish Book Award. His work has appeared in a number of books, including *Eleven Spanish Photographers, Zaragoza, Cáceres* and *Palacio Floral de Navarra.*

A Day in the Life of America 1986

Aaron Chang
American/San Diego, California
Chang is senior staff photographer for *Surfing* magazine. In 1982, he received the American Society of Magazine Photographers Award for Excellence and was named one of the top five sports photographers in the United States by *American Photographer* magazine. His work has appeared in *Newsweek, Stern, People* and *Gentlemen's Quarterly.*

Gary S. Chapman
American/Louisville, Kentucky
Chapman is a staff photographer for *The Louisville Courier-Journal Sunday Magazine* and a member of the Image Bank. His work has appeared in *National Geographic, Traveler, Time, Forbes, Newsweek* and *World.*

Paul Chesley
American/Aspen, Colorado
Chesley, a freelance photographer who has worked with the National Geographic Society since 1975, travels regularly to Europe and Asia. Solo exhibitions of his work have appeared at museums in London, Tokyo and New York. His work has also been seen in *Fortune, Time, Esquire, GEO* and *Stern.*

Rich Clarkson
American/Denver, Colorado
Clarkson was formerly director of photography for *National Geographic* and is a contributing photographer to *Sports Illustrated.* He was president of the National Press Photographers Association and has twice served as chairman of the Pictures of the Year competition. He has co-authored four books, and his work has appeared regularly in *Life, Time* and the *Saturday Evening Post,* among others.

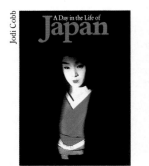

A Day in the Life of Japan 1985

Jodi Cobb
American/Washington, D.C.
Cobb, who has a master's degree from the University of Missouri, has been a staff photographer for *National Geographic* since 1977. She has photographed major articles on China, Jerusalem, Jordan and London. In 1985, she was named White House Photographer of the Year, the first female to be chosen. Cobb was the subject of the Public Broadcasting Service's television documentary "On Assignment."

Pedro Coll
Spanish/Palma de Mallorca
Coll is a freelance photographer who works in Spain for AGE FotoStock and for other photo agencies in England, Germany, the Middle East, Australia, the Far East, Central America, the Caribbean and the United States. He contributed to the UNESCO book *Patrimonio del Mundo*. A professional photographer since 1975, Coll specializes in geographic photography and has been on assignment in five continents.

J.D. Dallet
French/Málaga
Dallet, a freelance photographer, works for *Lookout* magazine (Spain), *Ifot* (Scandinavia) and *Uniphoto Press* (Japan). The Spanish Ministry of Tourism awarded him the Premio Nacional de Fotografía Turística and the Premio Santa María del Villar. He has exhibited at the National Museum of Denmark and in Málaga, Spain.

Anne Day
American/New York, New York
Day is a freelancer who previously photographed for *A Day in the Life of Japan* and *A Day in the Life of America*. Her pictures have been published in *Time, Newsweek, Fortune, The New York Times* and *Le Monde* as well as in several books on architecture. She has most recently worked in Haiti, Nicaragua and South Africa.

Carlos de Andrés

Madrid   1986

Carlos de Andrés
Spanish/Madrid
De Andrés works for the Spanish photo agency Cover. His photographs have been published in *Der Spiegel, Newsweek, Time, Bunte, Männer, Vogue, El País, Cambio 16, Diario 16, Interviú, Tiempo* and Fotopres Books. He received Fotopres awards in 1986 and 1987 and the Tradiciones Populares de España in 1986.

Arnaud de Wildenberg
French/Paris
A freelance photographer since 1984, de Wildenberg is best known for his coverage of Afghanistan and Iranian and Cambodian refugees. His Uganda coverage won him the *Paris Match* contest for news reporting in 1980. He also won an award from the World Press Photo Holland Foundation for his coverage of Poland's Lech Walesa.

Jay Dickman

A Day in the Life of America   1986

Jay Dickman
American/Denver, Colorado
A photographer who worked in the Dallas, Texas, area for 16 years, Dickman recently moved to Colorado. His work has appeared in *National Geographic, Life, Time, Newsweek, Bunte, Stern, GEO* and other publications. His awards include a Pulitzer Prize in 1983, first place in the World Press Photo competition and the Sigma Delta Chi Award as well as many state and regional awards.

Dan Dry
American/Louisville, Kentucky
Dry is a freelancer whose work has been published by *National Geographic, Time, Newsweek, Fortune, Town & Country* and *The New York Times*. He runs Dan Dry & Associates, which specializes in photography for annual reports and advertising for many Fortune 500 firms. He has won more than 300 awards and was recognized as the Newspaper Photographer of the Year in 1981.

Misha Erwitt
American/New York, New York
A native New Yorker, Erwitt has been taking pictures since he was 11 years old. He is a staff photographer for New York's *Daily News* and has also been published in *American Photographer, Esquire, People, Manhattan Inc.* and *USA Today*.

Terry Ferrante
American/New York, New York
Ferrante specializes in studio still-life photography for corporate clients including, *Newsweek*, Germaine Monteil, Black & Decker, Seiko watches, AT&T and Avon.

Gerrit Fokkema

Wilcannia, Australia   1983

Gerrit Fokkema
Australian/Sydney
Fokkema is a freelance photographer who concentrates on both corporate and editorial assignments. For 11 years he was on the staff of a number of Australian newspapers, including *The Sydney Morning Herald*. His work is in the collections of the Australian National Gallery, the New South Wales Art Gallery and the National Library.

Frank Fournier
French/New York, New York
Fournier's work has appeared in a broad array of magazines and journals, including *Time, Newsweek, Paris Match, Stern, Life* and *The Sunday Times Magazine* (London). The World Press Photo Holland Foundation awarded him the 1986 Press Photo of the Year award. Fournier is a member of Contact Press Images.

Raphaël Gaillarde
French/Paris
Gaillarde is a Gamma news photographer. His in-depth coverage of world events has appeared in many European magazines, including *GEO*.

Germán Gallego

Spain   1986

Germán Gallego
Spanish/Madrid
Gallego currently works for *Interviú* magazine and has also been employed by *Diario 16, La Vanguardia* and *Hola*. He has won a number of awards for his photography, including first prize from the Club Internacional de Prensa and two Fotopres awards.

Sam Garcia
American/New York, New York
Garcia has been a member of the Nikon Professional Services staff for more than 12 years. He trained the space shuttle astronauts in the use of 35-mm still equipment and photographed several launches. Garcia has also covered most major sporting events, including three Olympics. He has worked on three previous *Day in the Life* projects—Hawaii, Canada and America.

Cristina García Rodero

Amil, Spain   1979

Cristina García Rodero
Spanish/Madrid
García Rodero is a freelancer specializing in fine-art photography. Her work has been published in several magazines, including *Lookout* and *El País*. Previously a drawing teacher, she now teaches photography at the Facultad de Bellas Artes de la Universidad Complutense de Madrid, where she first studied Spanish fiestas, customs and traditions. In 1985, she was awarded the Premio Planeta de Fotografía.

Jerry Gay
American/Long Island, New York
Gay is a staff photographer at *Newsday* in Long Island, New York. Prior to that job he worked as a freelancer for clients including Time-Life Inc., Associated Press, *The Los Angeles Times, The New York Times* and *USA Today*. He has also taught photography and photojournalism at the Brooks Institute of Photography in Santa Barbara, California.

Georg Gerster
Swiss/Zürich
Gerster has been a freelance writer-photographer specializing in science since 1956. He received a Ph.D. in German literature and philology from the University of Zürich. Gerster frequently contributes to *National Geographic, Neue Zürcher Zeitung, The Sunday Times Magazine* (London) and *Omni*. He is working on a book of aerial photographs of American agriculture.

Diego Goldberg
Argentine/Buenos Aires
After beginning his photographic career in Latin America as a correspondent for Camera Press, Goldberg moved to Paris in 1977 as a Sygma staff photographer. His work has been featured in the world's major magazines. In 1984, he won a prize for feature photography in the World Press Photo competition.

Lynn Goldsmith
American/New York, New York
Goldsmith's work has appeared on the covers of *Life, Newsweek, Elle, Rolling Stone* and *People* magazines. Among her honors are awards from the World Press Photo competition, the Nikon International Photo contest and the Arles Recontres. She is the founding member of the LGI photo agency which specializes in contemporary celebrity portraiture.

Miguel González
Spanish/Madrid
González has been working for the photo agency Cover since 1981. His work has been published in *Interviú, Cambio 16, Tiempo, The New York Times, Newsweek, The Sunday Times Magazine* (London), *Paris Match, Figaro, Epoca, Stern, Bunte* and *Der Spiegel*, among others. In 1982, González was awarded first prize in the Fotopres competition, and from 1982 to 1986, he won six additional Fotopres awards.

Arthur Grace
American/Washington, D.C.
A staff photographer for *Newsweek* magazine, Grace has recently contributed *Newsweek* cover stories on New York Governor Mario Cuomo and comedian Robin Williams and has mounted a one-man exhibition of his black-and-white photographs. His work has been published in leading magazines worldwide during his 15-year association with the Sygma photo agency.

Skeeter Hagler
American/Dallas, Texas
Winner of the 1980 Pulitzer Prize for feature photography, Hagler has worked for *The Dallas Times Herald* for the past 13 years. After receiving a degree in architecture from the University of Texas in 1971, Hagler turned to photojournalism as a full-time career. Since then, he has won many state and national awards in the United States.

Dirck Halstead
American/Washington, D.C.
Halstead is a contract photographer for *Time* magazine. He previously was special roving photographer and Saigon bureau chief for United Press International. In addition to his work at *Time*, Halstead continues to take assignments for travel magazines. Among the honors he has received are the Robert Capa Award and the White House News Photographers Association Award.

Manuel Hernández de León

Madrid 1985

Manuel Hernández de León
Spanish/Madrid
Hernández de León has been working for the Spanish news agency EFE for 22 years, having started at the age of 13. He studied journalism at Madrid University and has had his work published in *The New York Times, Newsweek, Bunte, Der Spiegel* and major Spanish newspapers and magazines. He received World Press Photo awards in 1981, 1983 and 1984.

Fernando Herráez
Spanish/Madrid
Herráez teaches photography at the Universidad Popular de Alcobenas in Madrid. His photographs have been published in *El País, El Dominical* and *Interviú* in Spain, *Avenue* in Holland and *Objectif Reporter* in France. He began his career in 1973 doing industrial photography. Herráez is one of the founding members of the photo agency Cover.

Ethan Hoffman
American/New York, New York
Hoffman is a New York photojournalist whose work has appeared in *Life, The Sunday Times Magazine* (London), *Stern, Paris Match, The New York Times* and *Fortune.* His newest book of photographs, *Butoh: Dance of the Dark Soul,* about Japan, was published by Aperture in the fall of 1987. Hoffman is president of Archive Pictures.

Graciela Iturbide

Juchitán, Mexico 1986

Graciela Iturbide
Mexican/Mexico City
Iturbide uses her camera to capture poetry in life. She has published two books in Mexico and has exhibited her work in Paris, Zürich and the United States.

Frank Johnston
American/Washington, D.C.
Johnston began his career with United Press International photographing the Kennedy assassination, the civil rights movement and the Vietnam War. In 1968, he joined *The Washington Post,* where he now covers national news. Johnston co-authored *The Working White House* and *Jonestown Massacre.* Among many other honors, he has won, three times, the Photographer of the Year Award presented by the White House News Photographers Association. In 1983, he received an Alicia Patterson fellowship to cover social and economic change in America.

Robb Kendrick
American/Houston, Texas
A freelance photographer since 1985, Kendrick takes on a mixture of corporate and editorial assignments. As an intern at *National Geographic,* he worked on an extended project in Washington and Oregon for *Traveler* magazine. Kendrick's work has appeared in *U.S. News & World Report, Forbes, Cosmopolitan, Business Week, National Geographic* and *GEO.*

David Hume Kennerly
American/Los Angeles, California
Winner of the Pulitzer Prize in 1972 for his feature photography in Vietnam, Kennerly was the official White House photographer for President Ford from 1974 to 1977. Kennerly was also awarded the Overseas Press Club's Olivier Rebbot Award in 1986. He is currently a contract photographer for *Time* magazine. In addition to writing his autobiography, *Shooter,* Kennerly has directed a 30-minute dramatic film, "Bao Chi," for the American Film Institute.

Douglas Kirkland
Canadian/Los Angeles, California
Kirkland is one of the world's best-known glamour and personality photographers. During 25 years in the business he has worked with Marilyn Monroe, Judy Garland, Barbra Streisand and Christie Brinkley. He was one of the founding members of Contact Press Images and is now with the Sygma photo agency.

Steve Krongard
American/New York, New York
Krongard's work ranges from the real to the fantastic, both on location and in the studio. His advertising and corporate clients include American Express, IBM, Kodak, AT&T, Polaroid and many others. His editorial pictures have appeared in most major magazines.

Kaku Kurita
Japanese/Tokyo
Kurita began his career as a commercial photographer, but in 1964, at the Tokyo Olympics, he turned to photojournalism. One of Japan's most successful international photojournalists, he works for *Time, Newsweek, The New York Times* and major publications throughout the world. He has been with Gamma in Tokyo for 13 years.

Jean-Pierre Laffont
French/New York, New York
Laffont attended the prestigious School of Graphic Arts in Vevey, Switzerland, prior to serving in the French Army during the Algerian War. He is a founding member of the Gamma USA and Sygma photo agencies. Since 1973, he has been a partner at Sygma. The New York Newspaper Guild and the Overseas Press Club of America have honored Laffont, and he has received the Madelein Dane Ross Award, the World Press Photo General Picture Award and the World Understanding Award. His work appears regularly in the world's leading news magazines.

Daniel Lainé
French/Paris
A professional photographer for 11 years, Lainé started as a freelancer for *Liberation* and has worked for *Partir* and *Grand Reportages* doing travel stories on South America and Africa. He was a correspondent in western and central Africa for Agence France-Presse and since 1981 has been a staff photographer for *Actuel.*

Frans Lanting

A Day in the Life of America 1986

Frans Lanting
Dutch/Santa Cruz, California
A freelancer who works for *National Geographic, GEO* and other magazines, Lanting has written several books and has received awards in World Press Photo, Pictures of the Year and American Society of Magazine Photographers competitions.

Sarah Leen

Beirut 1985

Sarah Leen
American/Philadelphia, Pennsylvania
A graduate of the University of Missouri, Leen has been on the staff of *The Philadelphia Inquirer* for five years, covering stories in Monaco, Lebanon and South Africa. For the past three years, she has taught at the Missouri Photo Workshop. In 1986, she received an honorable mention in the Robert F. Kennedy awards competition for her story on Alzheimer's disease.

Andy Levin

New York 1982

Andy Levin
American/New York, New York
Levin is a magazine photojournalist living in New York City. His photographs have appeared in various magazines, including *Life, National Geographic, People* and *Parade.* His subjects have ranged from Nebraska farmers to rap musicians. Levin was awarded top honors in the Pictures of the Year competition in both 1985 and 1986.

Barry Lewis
British/London
A freelance photographer for the last 11 years, Lewis has received awards from the Arts Council and *Vogue* magazine and is a founding member of the Network photo agency. His photographic essays have been published in such major magazines as *GEO, The Sunday Times Magazine* (London) and *The Observer.*

John Loengard
American/New York, New York
Loengard joined the staff of *Life* magazine in 1961. He has photographed dozens of essays, on such subjects as Georgia O'Keeffe, the Shakers and cowboys. When *Life* was revived in 1978, he was named picture editor. Loengard was the first picture editor of *People* magazine. In 1982, his essay on photographers, "Shooting Past 80," was awarded first prize for a picture story in the Pictures of the Year competition. Loengard teaches and lectures on photojournalism. His first book, *Pictures Under Discussion,* was published by Amphoto in March 1987.

Gerd Ludwig
West German/New York, New York
A founding member of Visum photo agency in Hamburg, Ludwig contributes regularly to *GEO, Life, Zeit Magazin, Stern, Fortune* and other magazines. He is a member of Deutsche Gesellschaft für Fotografie.

Mary Ellen Mark
American/New York, New York
The winner of numerous awards and grants, Mark has exhibited and published her work the world over. In 1985, she won the Robert F. Kennedy Award and in 1986, the Phillipe Halsman Award for Photojournalism from the American Society of Magazine Photographers. Her work appears regularly in *Life, The Sunday Times Magazine* (London), *Stern, Vanity Fair* and *The New York Times.*

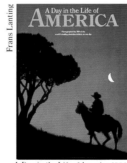

Stephanie Maze

A Day in the Life of Japan 1985

Stephanie Maze
American/Rio de Janeiro
Since 1979, Maze has been a freelance photographer for *National Geographic* and has worked in the United States, Mexico, Spain, Portugal, Costa Rica, Puerto Rico and Brazil. She has covered three Olympic Games and is currently working in Latin America for numerous American and foreign publications

Wally McNamee
American/Washington, D.C.
During his 30-year career as a photographer, McNamee has worked for *The Washington Post* and *Newsweek*, to which he has contributed more than 100 covers. He is a four-time winner of the Photographer of the Year Award from the White House News Photographers Association, and has received many other honors.

Dilip Mehta
Canadian/Toronto, Ontario
A member of Contact Press Images, Mehta has covered events in India, Pakistan, the United States, Afghanistan and numerous other countries. Mehta's pictorial essays have been published in *Time, Newsweek, GEO, Bunte, The New York Times, Paris Match, Figaro* and *The Sunday Times Magazine* (London). He has won two first prizes from the World Press Photo Holland Foundation and an award from the Overseas Press Club.

Doug Menuez
American/San Francisco, California
Menuez is a contract photographer with *USA Today* and a member of the Picture Group agency. He shoots regularly for *Time, Newsweek, U.S. News & World Report, Forbes, Business Week,* and other publications. After graduating with a degree in photojournalism from San Francisco State University, Menuez was a photo intern at *The Washington Post.*

Claus C. Meyer
West German/Rio de Janeiro
Meyer works for the Black Star photo agency. In 1985, he was selected by *Communication World* as one of the top 10 annual report photographers in the world. His color work has been recognized by Kodak and Nikon, and in 1981 he won the Nikon International Great Prize. He has published several books on Brazil.

New York   1981

Maddy Miller
American/New York, New York
Currently assistant picture editor for *People* magazine, Miller was previously assistant picture editor and a staff photographer for *US* magazine. Prior to that, she was a freelance photographer. Miller began her career at *Look* in 1966, and her work has been published in many major magazines.

Carlos Monge
Spanish/Madrid
Monge is the photo editor and a staff photographer for *Diario 16,* the Madrid daily. He was previously a photographer for the weekly magazine *Cambio 16,* which he joined in 1976. Monge studied engraving at the National Graphics School in Madrid before becoming a photographer. In 1984, he won a Fotopres Award.

A Day in the Life of Canada   1984

Robin Moyer
American/Hong Kong
Moyer is a *Time* magazine photographer based in Hong Kong. In 1982, he won the Press Photo of the Year Award from the World Press Photo competition and a citation from the Overseas Press Club for his coverage of the Lebanon conflict.

Carlos Navajas
Spanish/Madrid
A professional freelance photographer since 1982, Navajas has worked for the tourist offices of Morocco and Tunisia and a variety of magazines, including *Departures, Fortune, Expression, The International Herald Tribune, El País* and *GEO.* His work has been honored by *Communication Arts Photography Annual* and *Creativity* magazine.

Matthew Naythons
American/San Francisco, California
A working journalist and physician, Naythons has spent most of his career alternating between covering world events and performing emergency room duty in San Francisco. In 1979, he founded an emergency medical team to care for Cambodian and Thai refugees. His photographs appear regularly in major magazines.

THE WALL

The Wall   1987

Seny Norasingh
American/Raleigh, North Carolina
Norasingh does freelance work for *National Geographic.* He previously photographed for *The Raleigh News and Observer, The Gastonia Gazette* and *The Daily Advance.* He was twice named North Carolina News Photographer of the Year.

Michael O'Brien
American/New York, New York
A native of Memphis, Tennessee, O'Brien began his career at *The Miami News,* where his work was recognized with two Robert F. Kennedy awards for outstanding coverage of the disadvantaged. His photography appears frequently in *Life, GEO* and other magazines.

Graeme Outerbridge
Bermudian/Southampton
Named the 1985 Young Outstanding Person of the Year in Bermuda, Outerbridge has exhibited his work in New York, Washington, D.C., London, Boston and Helsinki. His photographs have been published in a variety of magazines, including *Vogue* and *The New Yorker.* His first book was *Bermuda Abstracts,* and he is currently working on a book about bridges.

Bernardo Pérez
Spanish/Madrid
Since 1978, Pérez has been a staff photographer for the Spanish daily *El País.* His work has also appeared in such foreign magazines as *Time, Newsweek* and *Stern.* Co-author of the book *250 Photographers in Spain,* he has been published in *Foto Profesional* magazine and Fotopres catalogues. Pérez has won three Fotopres awards.

Bill Pierce
American/New York, New York
Pierce is a contract photographer for *Time* magazine and is represented by the international photo agency Sygma. A Princeton graduate, he won the 1983 Overseas Press Club Olivier Rebbot Award for his photo reporting in Belfast and Beirut. Pierce's work has appeared in *Life, Paris Match, The New York Times* and *Stern* magazines, in addition to *Time.*

Larry C. Price
American/Philadelphia, Pennsylvania
Price is the director of photography for *The Philadelphia Inquirer Sunday Magazine.* He previously worked for *The El Paso Times* and *The Fort Worth Star-Telegram.* Since beginning his photography career in 1977, Price has won two Pulitzer Prizes—in 1981 for coverage of the Liberian coup and in 1985 for photographs of Angola and El Salvador. Price's work has also been honored by the Overseas Press Club, the World Press Photo Holland Foundation and the National Press Photographers Association.

Roger Ressmeyer
American/San Francisco, California
A Yale graduate, Ressmeyer has photographed cover and feature stories for *Smithsonian, People, Time, Newsweek* and *Life.* His work has also appeared on the covers of dozens of books whose authors include Shirley MacLaine, Danielle Steel, Patti Davis and John DeLorean. The founder of Starlight photo studio in San Francisco, Ressmeyer has won numerous awards for his portraiture as well as for his coverage of high technology and fashion.

Jim Richardson
American/Denver, Colorado
A special projects photographer for *The Denver Post,* Richardson has published essays on his native state of Kansas in *Life, American Photographer* and *Country Journal.* He was given special recognition in the World Understanding Award competition in 1975, 1976 and 1977.

Bilbao, Spain   1986

Juantxu Rodríguez
Spanish/Madrid
Rodríguez has worked for the Spanish photo agency Cover. His photographs have appeared in *La Vanguardia, El País, Cambio 16, Le Figaro, The New York Times* and *Newsweek.* He has received several Fotopres awards and has exhibited throughout Spain.

Benito Román
Spanish/Madrid
A freelancer, Román works for *El País, Panorama, Hombre de Hoy, Futuro* and *Dinero.* His photographs have also been published in *Hermano Lobo, Diario 16* and *Gaceta Ilustrada.* In Paris he worked for Agence Sipa-Presse. He is the recipient of a 1986 Fotopres award.

Galen Rowell
American/San Francisco, California
Rowell is an environmental photojournalist who has written and photographed seven large-format books as well as having done assignments for such magazines as *National Geographic* and *Sports Illustrated.* He received the 1984 Ansel Adams Award for landscape photography and has had numerous one-man shows, including a three-month exhibit at the Smithsonian Institution in 1987. His most recent book is *Mountain Light: In Search of the Dynamic Landscape.*

Madrid   1985

Robert Royal
American/Madrid
Alabama-born Royal has lived in Madrid for nearly two decades. A professional photographer since 1975, he has taken pictures for *Time, The New York Times,* De Beers and Comunidad de Madrid. He continues to do a mix of corporate and editorial photography.

Angel Ruiz de Azúa
Spanish/Bilbao
Chief photo editor of the Basque newspaper *Deía* since 1980, Ruiz de Azúa has been working for newspapers since he was 14 years old. His photos have been published in *Paris Match, Interviú* and a variety of other magazines, and he has worked for the news agencies UPI and EFE. He was awarded the Premio Planeta de Fotoperiodismo in 1984.

Sebastião Salgado
Brazilian/Paris
An international economist by training, Salgado is associated with the Magnum photo agency. His work has appeared in *Time, Paris Match, Stern, The Sunday Times Magazine* (London) and *Fortune.* His ongoing study of the indigenous peoples of Latin America was recognized with a W. Eugene Smith grant in 1982. He also won a World Press Photo award in 1984 for his coverage of Ethiopia. In 1986, his latest book, *The Other America,* was published.

Al Satterwhite
American/New York, New York
Satterwhite began shooting professional press assignments while still in college. Since he became a full-time photographer, his work has been published in *Time, Newsweek, Sports Illustrated* and *Life* magazines. In 1975, he was selected for *Who's Who in Photography*. In 1979, he moved to New York to branch into corporate and advertising photography.

Alberto Schommer
Spanish/Madrid
Schommer does freelance work for *El País* and several other Spanish and international publications. He is the recipient of three awards in Spain, and his work has been exhibited there and abroad. He has co-authored a number of books, including *Los Reyes Viajan, Retratos Psicológicos* and *El Grito de un Pueblo*, and has produced one on his own entitled *Máscaras, Fermento, Civilizaciones*.

Barcelona   1986

Marta Sentís
Spanish/Barcelona
Sentís is a freelancer specializing in photojournalism and still photos for movies. Her work has been published in *El País, La Vanguardia, Cambio 16, Interviú* and *Diario 16*. She has also done assignments for the United Nations. In recent years, Sentís has focused on Egypt and on African and Caribbean immigrants in industrialized nations.

Dover, Reino Unido   1984

Neal Slavin
American/New York, New York
The recipient of numerous awards, Slavin is published regularly in *The Sunday Times Magazine* (London), *Stern, GEO, Town & Country, Newsweek* and *Connoisseur*. His work has appeared in one-man and group shows. His latest book is *Britons*.

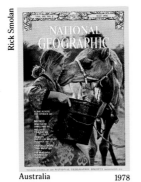
Australia   1978

Rick Smolan
American/New York, New York
Co-director of *A Day in the Life of Spain*, Smolan also created *A Day in the Life of Australia* (1981), *A Day in the Life of Hawaii* (1983), *A Day in the Life of Canada* (1984), *A Day in the Life of Japan* (1985) and *A Day in the Life of America* (1986). Prior to these extravaganzas, Smolan was a full-time photojournalist whose work appeared in such major publications as *Time* and *National Geographic*.

Andrew Stawicki
Polish/Toronto, Ontario
After working as a staff photographer in Frankfurt for *Bild Zeitung* and in Warsaw for *Swiatowid*, Stawicki joined *The Toronto Star* in 1983. He has won several prizes in Poland and Holland and has exhibited his work in Poland and Canada.

Ivory Coast   1980

Víctor Steinberg
Spanish/Madrid
Before taking his present job as staff photographer for *Cambio 16*, Steinberg was a correspondent in Spain for Gamma. His photos have been published in *Newsweek, Time, Le Point, L'Express, Stern* and *Bunte*. In the early 1970s, he taught history at the University of Buenos Aires. Steinberg has received the Premio Planeta and Fotopres awards.

George Steinmetz
American/San Francisco, California
Before graduating from Stanford University with a degree in geophysics, Steinmetz dropped out to spend two and a half years hitchhiking through more than 20 African countries. His work appears regularly in *Fortune, Forbes, GEO, Mother Jones* and *The New York Times Magazine*. He is currently photographing oil exploration for *National Geographic*.

London   1980

Antonio Suárez
Spanish/Madrid
Suárez is affiliated with the Sygma photo agency and specializes in news and portrait photography. He was previously associated with the Gamma and Sunset agencies. His work has been published by *Cambio 16, Tiempo, Interviú, El País, La Vanguardia, Newsweek, Der Spiegel, Time, Paris Match* and *Nouvel Observateur*. He was the recipient of a Fotopres award in 1983.

Patrick Tehan
American/Santa Ana, California
Tehan is on the staff of *The Orange County Register* in Santa Ana, California. A photo published in *A Day in the Life of America* earned him top honors in the magazine division of the Pictures of the Year competition. In 1981, Tehan was named Regional Photographer of the Year by the National Press Photographers Association.

Tomasz Tomaszewski
Polish/Cambridge, Massachusetts
Tomaszewski is vice-president of the Union of Polish Art Photographers. His work has appeared in many international publications, including *National Geographic, Paris Match, Stern, Domenica Christiana* and *La Vie*. His book, *Remnants—The Last Jews of Poland*, was published in Switzerland in 1981 and in the United States in 1986. His photographs have been exhibited in Poland, France, Sweden, Canada and the United States. He has won several prizes in Poland and France.

David C. Turnley
American/Detroit, Michigan
Turnley has been a *Detroit Free Press* staff photographer since 1980. He is now working on a project about Afrikaners for *National Geographic* and the *Detroit Free Press*. He has won several Overseas Press Club awards and in 1986 won three World Press Photo awards for his foreign coverage.

Peter Turnley
American/Paris
Turnley is a contract photographer in Paris for *Newsweek*, covering Europe, the USSR, North Africa and the Middle East. He has published one book, *A Food Lover's Guide to Paris*, and has received several French photography awards. In 1986, he was cited by the Overseas Press Club for his international coverage. Turnley studied at the University of Michigan, the Sorbonne and the Institut d'Etudes Politiques in Paris before becoming a photographer.

Neal Ulevich
American/Beijing
Ulevich is a staff photographer and the photo editor for the Associated Press in China. He has worked in Asia for 17 years, covering news events throughout the region. His photographs of a violent political upheaval in Bangkok, taken when he lived in Thailand, won him the 1977 Pulitzer Prize for news photography.

Jerry Valente
American/New York, New York
Valente specializes in hotel advertising, but his work includes editorial and corporate assignments and industrial annual reports. His photos have appeared in *A Day in the Life of America*, and he hopes awards await him in the future.

France   1985

John Vink
Belgian/Paris
A member of Agence Vu in Paris, Vink has been a freelance photographer since 1971. His work has appeared in *Time, Le Monde* and *Liberation*. He is currently involved with personal projects on Italy and the African Sahel. His photographs have appeared in 30 group and solo shows in Europe. In 1986, he was the recipient of a W. Eugene Smith grant.

Wendy Watriss
American/Houston, Texas
Watriss is a photojournalist associated with the Woodfin Camp photo agency. Her work has been published in *Life, GEO, The New York Times, Stern, Photoreportages, Smithsonian, The Village Voice, Newsweek, Mother Jones* and *The Christian Science Monitor*. Prior to turning to professional photography in 1971, Watriss was a producer of documentaries for National Educational Television.

David H. Wells
American/Philadelphia, Pennsylvania
Wells is a freelance photojournalist whose work has appeared in *GEO, Life, The Los Angeles Times, National Geographic, Newsweek, The New York Times, Time, USA Today* and *U.S. News & World Report*. He was previously a staff photographer for the Syracuse Newspapers and a contract photographer for *The Los Angeles Times*. In 1985, he was the recipient of a Society of Newspaper Design Award.

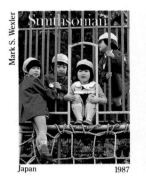
Japan   1987

Mark S. Wexler
American/New York, New York
Wexler travels the world as a photographer for a variety of editorial and corporate clients, including *Time, Life, Smithsonian* and *GEO*. He has won three World Press Photo awards for his work on *A Day in the Life of Japan*.

Ramón Zabalza
Spanish/Madrid
Zabalza has specialized in documentary photography in Spain since 1973. His pictures have been shown in solo and group exhibitions in Spain and Germany. He recently worked on a photo essay on gypsies in Madrid.

Friends, Advisors and Consultants

Jesús Abad González
Dolores Abolghasemi
Antonio and Mates Acosta
Julio Agosti
Ana Aguado Puig
María José Aguiló García
Consuelo Aguirre Ramírez
Ritxi Aizpuru
Germán Alarcón Martín
María Luisa Albacar i Gelaber
Rafaela Alcántara
Miguel Alemán Castillo
Oswaldo Alonso
Juan Angel Alonso Alonso
Pedro Alonso Gallego
María Pilar Alonso Granja
Miguel Angel Alústixa Zubiri
Manuel Alvarez
Carlos Alvarez Alonso
Ramón Alvarez Argüelles
Manuel Alvarez Barrios
Maite Alvarez Peinado
Don Alvaro
Ignacio Ameztoy
Carlos de Andrés
Bitor Aranzábal
Jordi Arasa Cuevas
Fidel and María Teresa Arejita
Juan Jesús Arejita
Mario Arellano García
Jaime Arias
Miguel Arias
Inmaculada Armicén
Begoña Arregui
Juanita Arreguiz
José Arrivi García
Pascual Asensio
Pabi Astondoa
Dorothea Auberger
Mario Ayuso
Andrés Aznar Alvarez
Ana Badía Belmonte
Lali Badosa
Ana Barasoaín
Gloria Barba Bernabeu
Pascual Barberán
Agustín Barrenechea-Arando
Dulce Barrios
Magdaleno Bausela
Javier Baviano Hernández
David Bell
Cindy Bellamy
Paloma Belles
Angel Bellido Amorós
Juan Mari Beloki
Jaume Beneit
Felisa Bengoetxea
Angel and Joan Berenguer
Gussie Bergerman
Agustín Betancor
Kathleen Bibbins
Princess Anne Marie Bismarck
Britt Blaser
Gene Blumberg
Abe H. Blumenfeld
Alfredo Bobillo
Captain Enrique Bohígas Jaime

Fermín Bohórquez
Bonifacio
Miguel Booth
Rafael Borràs
Carlos Bosch
Vicente Bostillo Greciano
Javier Boter Sans
Babeth Bousquet
Nigel Bowden
Erik Boyd
Bob Breeden
George and Bettina Brown
David Brown
Luis Brox Delgado
Humphrey Bruno
Eduardo Bustamante Fernández
Rosario Caballero Castro
Francisco Cadenas Fernández
Antonio Calavera
Juan Caldentey
Germán Calvillo Urabayen
Ildefonso Calvo
Lourdes Camarasa
Roseta Campos
François Camus
Juan Canals Ferres
Esperanza Caneda
Antonio Cañete López
Nicolás Canto de Andrés
Mercedes Caravantes
Fabriciano Carballo
Ken Carbone
Angel Carchenilla
Mother Superior Matilde
   Carrascal
María Angustias Carrascosa
María Carretero Goizueta
David Carriere
Marimar Carrión
Maru Casado
Juan Casas
Jacqueline Cassagne
Eva Castro
Juan Castro
Rosario Castro
Gustavo Catalán
Alvaro Chinchetru Fernández de
   Alegría
Guadalupe Chinea
Judy Ann Christensen
Becky Christiansen
Albert Chu
Jesse and Rhonda Claman
Luis Cobos
Daniel Cohen
Gail Cohen
Janice Cohen
Norman and Hannah Cohen
Ramón Colom
Rafael Coloma Aramburu
Sandy Colton
Vicki Comiskey
Francisco Conde
Teodoro Conde Minaya
Carmen Cordeiro
Mariana Cores Gomendio
Jack Corn
Pedro Corral
Luis Cortés
Manuel Cortés Magán
Santiago Costa
Manuel Criado Carreja
Robert Cromer
Emilio de la Cruz
Eduardo Cuevas Fernández
Maxine Curry
José María Cuspinera

Don Davidson
Robyn Davidson
Paul Delaney
Ray DeMoulin
Javier Deobarro Hernández
Brigitte Dern
Ana Díaz Gabaraín
Carmelo Díaz Ropero
Carmelo Díaz del Ruiz
Geoffrey Dobson
Beltrán Domecq
Mercedes Domecq Ybarra
Manuel Domecq Zurita
Adolfo Domínguez
Mary Donovan
Gene and Gayle Driskell
Natasha Driskell
Robert Earl
Alvaro Echebarría
Julián Echeberría
María Echeberría
Suzanna Echeberría
Julián Echevarría
María Teresa Echevarría
Jesús Echezarreta
Luis Vicente Elías
José María Elías Pastor
Alberto Elordi
Joseba Elósegui
Andrés Encinas
Luis Enríquez de Andrés
María José Enríquez de Luna
Elliott Erwitt
Juan Escandell
Gladys Esparza Gargurevich
Barbara Essick
Manuel Esteban
Manolo Estepa
José Manuel Ester Fernández
José Luis Estévez
Enrike Etxebarría
Santos Etxebarría
José Luis Fabá Soldevila
Harlan Felt
Fermín
Bernardo Fernández
Carlos Fernández
Elvira Fernández
Julio Fernández
Miguel Fernández
María Luisa Fernández Bernabé
Esther Fernández Iñigo
Lourdes Fernández Trillo
Juan Fernández-Armesto
Esperanza Fernández-Mayoralas
   Alarcón
Armando Fernández-Xexta
Terry Ferrante
The Bienvenido Ferrer family
Abdelwahid Fikri
Kristin Fiske
Alex Fletcher
Liz Francis
Piedad Frías Nogales
Miguel Fujiwara
John Fulton
Gonzalo Galiano Casas
Fernando Gallardo

Angeles García
Aurora García
Manuel García
Marina García
Juan García Alonso
César García Arribas
Manuel García Bastida
Francisco García Castelló
José Luis García González
Jesús García Gorbea
María Luisa García Martínez
María de la Salud García
   Martínez
Lieutenant Colonel García
   Muñoz
Tomás García Recio
José García Reyes
Rodolfo García Serrano
Rogelio García Suárez
Michel M. Garnier
Carlos María Gil
Dan Gilbert
Jesús Esteban Ginto
Remei Giralt
Paolo Girelli
Francisco Girón
Russell Glick
Jon Goikoetxea
Mayte Goizueta
Lieutenant Colonel José Luis
   Gómez Ezquerro
The Felipe González family
Victoria González
Yolanda González
The González Roda family
María Victoria Gorbeña
Lidia Gorrón
Josie de Goytisolo
Will Gray
John Griebsch
Francisco and Isabel Guirola
   García
Fernando Gutiérrez
José Luis Gutiérrez
José Luis Gutiérrez Lizárraga
Elena Gutiérrez-Bolívar
Commander and Mrs. Peter Hall
John Hazlett
Alberto Heras Pérez
José Heredia Maya
Agustín Hernández
José Hernández
Roberto Hernández
Rosario Hernández
Lourdes Hernández Gil
Mariano S. Hernández González
Luis Hernando de Larramendi
Manuel Herranz
Salvador Hevia
Dennis Hextell
Carmen Heymann
Will Hooper
Will Hopkins
Karen Horace
Richard Horowitz
Stephen Hull
Agustín Ibarrola
Julián Iglesias
Manuel Iglesias Fernández
Vern Iuppa
Derek Ive
Ken Jacobs
Carmen Jaime
Kenneth and Evelyn Janello
Juan Jiménez
Luis Jiménez
Pilar Jiménez

rificación Jiménez Sánchez
eve Jobs
ancy Jones
ico Junquera
rraine Kacaba
ane Kay
mes Klein
ynthia Kling-Jones
ndrew Kruger
afael Labón
erek and Diane Lambert
illiam Lane
aría Larisch, Countess of
  Salamanca
ristina Larrinanga
ernando León Peña
artin Levin
awrence Ley
erónica Líbano
en Lieberman
sé Antonio Lillo Amador
sé Antonio Linares
ark Little
steban Llagostera
ntonio Llatas
uim Llenas
urxo Lobato
ntonio López
sús López
sé Luis López
oberto López
sé María López Agueda
rancisca López de Gutiérrez
an José López Marriqi
armen López Mateos
enito López Sánchez
ichard Lorant
sús Pedro Lorente
olores Luca de Tena
epa Luke
uth Mackay
harlotte Mackenzie
osé Magariño
uan Luis Manfredi
ernando Manso Borra
eresa Manzano Nieto
velyn Mariperisena
losén Ignacio Marqués
aquín Marqués
nastasio Martín
onsuelo Martín
fari-Carmen Martín
ictorino Martín
ablo Martín Cantalejo
na Martín Gamero
milio Martín Manzanas
Mike Marshall
ntonio Martín Méndez
milia Martínez
María del Pilar Martínez
edro L. Martínez
ogelio Martínez
uenny Martínez de Campos
ndrés Martínez Díaz
uan Martínez Guijarro

Colonel Martínez Ortiz
Antonio Martínez Simó
Carmen Martínez de Sola
Richard and Lucienne Matthews
The Mayor, El Cerro de
  Andévalo
Rafael Mazarrasa
Jack McTaggart
Helena Medina
The Jesús Menargues family
José Mari Mendizábal
José Vicente Merino
Vicente Merino
Princess Smilja Mihailovitch
Glen Minnard
Juan J. Mintegui
Pam Miracle
Miguel Mohedo Canales
Joaquín Molina y Fernández de
  los Ríos
Manuel Molinero
Arturo and Alicia Molino Suárez
Arantxa Mongelos
Francisco Javier Mongelos
Art Mont
Dominga Montado Barbosa
Alberto Montagut
Eduardo Montuil Fernández de
  Córdoba
Jaime de Mora y Aragón
Juan Morales Bastos
Concha Morell
Joaquín Moreno
José María Moreno Carrascal
Alonso Moreno de Silva
Miguel Morer
Ann Moscicki
Bruce Mowery
Luis Moya
The Mozarab family
Kai Mui
Karen Mullarkey
Mari-Carmen Muñoz Andrés
Mercedes Murillo
Lon Murphy
Jesús Muruaga
Julio Muruaga
Remedios N. del Río
Carmela Naval
Diego Navarrete
Coro Navarro
María Navarro
Francisco Negrín
Lois Nettell
Ada Marina Newman
Susana Nieva Soto
José Luis Nocito
Jesús Novela Berlin
Amelia Noriega
Rita Nuez Fuentes
Rodrigo Núñez
Jaime Ollé
Tim O'Meara
Antonio Ordóñez
Manolita Orejas
Albi Ortega
Pilar Ortega
José Ortiz de Solórzano
Manuel Ortuño
Eva Orúe
Dan O'Shea
Mercedes Ouro
Edward Owen

Agustín Padrón Mesa
Iris Pagano de Dornier
Carmen Palacios
José Palacios
Guillermo Palanca Ussía
Guy Palmer
Alfonso S. Palomares
Jesús and José Pallaruelo
Mari-Carmen Parada
Eduardo Paramio Roca
Enrique Paredes
Ann Pasque
María Paz Sáenz
José Peralta Aparicio
José María Perea Soro
Amanda Pérez
Tomás Pérez
José and María Pérez
Manuel Pérez Flores
Manuel Pérez Illescas
Hernán Pérez del Pulgar
Alfonso Pérez Sánchez
Carlos Pérez Siquier
Mercedes Pérez de Villaamil
Guillermo Pérez Villalata
Elizabeth Perle
Mario Perrone
Donald Person
Agustín Petri Hernández
Manuel Pinto
Carl Pite
Braulio Pitera
Charles A. Plummer
Betina Pons
Cristina Ponte Cullen
Elizabeth Pope
Germán Porras Olalla
Dwight Porter
José Porto Matalobos
Carmen Posada Moreno
Carol Potok
Miguel Povedán
Joan Powell
Herman Prior
Joaquín Pujol
Cherie Quaintance
Gerardo Quintana
Luis Rábade
Bernardo Ramos
Isidro Ramos
Miguel Ramos
Sonya Raschart
Ricardo Reguera Fernández
Spencer Reiss
Reprocolor Llovet, S.A.
ReproColor USA Ltd.
Josefina Revilla
Antonio Rey
José Andrés del Rey Manzano
Luis Rey-Stolle de Imbert
The Jesús da Ribeira family
Catalina Ríos Sánchez
Rafael Roa Fernández
Fernando Robaina
Rodney Robson
Eduardo Roca
Adelita Rocha
Angel Rodríguez
Conchita Rodríguez
Juan José Rodríguez
Juantxu Rodríguez
Mari-Carmen Rodríguez
Commander Enrique Rodríguez
  Gelindo
Albino Rodríguez López

Uri Ruiz Bikandi
Manuel Ruiz Hernández
Apolonio Ruiz Ligero
Antonio Ruiz Vega
Paz Sáenz Ruiz-Zorrilla
Joaquim Sabriá
Francisca Sadornil
Aurelio Sahagún
Enrique Sáiz
Nicolás Salces Fernández
Pep Salvat
José Luis Samaranch
Marianne Samenko
Begoña Sánchez
Fernando Sánchez
Luis Sánchez Nieto
Ramón Sánchez Reyes
José María de Sanmillán
Javier Santamaría Zabalza
Jaime Sanz
Esteban Saralegui Zabaleta
Tomás Sárate Cologan
Toni Sardá
Imam Abdul Sattar Khan
Enrique Saúl Vuelta
Steve Scheier
Fred Scherrer
Diego Scherscheanski
Henrik Scherscheanski
Pablo Scherscheanski
Patrick Scherscheanski
Rosario Scherscheanski
Birgit Schirmeier
Leonard Sclafani
John Scully
Miguel Segovia Merelo
Bernabé Seguro
Mireia Sentís
María del Carmen Serrano
  Altimiras
Kay Sexton
Robert Shanebrook
Agustín Shushei Yamada
Dora and Domingo Simón
Bob Siroka
Richard Smith
Temple Smith
Leslie Smolan
Marvin and Gloria Smolan
Sandy Smolan
Inmaculada Soarín
Luis Soler
Ramón de la Sota
Alfonso Soto Beobide
The Francisco Soto Iborra family
Teresa Soto Ortego
Florentino Sotomayor Basabe
Joseph Strear
Francisco Suárez
Jaime Suárez
Jaime Suárez Fernández
Odette Suárez de Puga
Ralph Subbiondo
Salvador Sueiro
Sylvia, Ari and Mies Surdoval
Kare Susan
Yusei Suzuki
Antonio Tejada Olmos
Garbine and Karmele Tellería
Lieutenant Federico Tena
Pedro Tomé Alonso
Gabriel Tomé Cerreiro
Antonio de Toro
Yolanda Torres
Francisco Torres Tercero

Michael Tschao
Pilar Uruñuela
Jontxu Urutxurtu Bengoetxea
Louis Urvois
Arantxa Ustarroz
Tina Vader
Emilio Valanzo
Manolo de Valdivia
Luis Valverde
Della Van Heyst
Carlos Vaquero
María Victoria Varela
Bárbara Vasallo
Belén Vasallo
Alberto Vasallo Tomé
Félix Vázquez
Francisco Vázquez
Raúl Vázquez
Carlos Vazuero
Bartolomé Vergara
Julián Vergés
Juan Vericad
Pilar Vico
Lolila and Mito Vidal
Angel Vigil
Miguel Vila Nuri
Jaume Vilamala
Mateo Villena
Miguel Angel Viñas
Jane Walker
Conchita Wallace
Cristina Wallace
Román Wang
Matthew Wells
Ken Welsh
Stephanie Whitmont
Marta Williams
Rosalind Williams Calabuig
Dave Winer
Matthew Winokur
Peter Workman
Robin Wu
Larry and Linda Wyner
Ramón Yáñez
Felisa Zabalaurtena
José Zafra Balverde
Captain Vicente Zaragoza
María Teresa Zubizarreta
Julián and Gillian de Zulueta

And very special thanks to
Ignacio Vasallo, without whom
this book would not have
been possible